Forestry Field Studies

A MANUAL FOR SCIENCE TEACHERS

By David D. Glenn and Donald I. Dickmann

Forestry Field Studies
A MANUAL FOR SCIENCE TEACHERS

NSTApress
National Science Teachers Association
Arlington, Virginia

National Science Teachers Association

Claire Reinburg, Director
Jennifer Horak, Managing Editor
Andrew Cocke, Senior Editor
Judy Cusick, Senior Editor
Wendy Rubin, Associate Editor

ART AND DESIGN
Will Thomas, Jr., Director—Cover and Interior Design
Cover photo by AVTG for iStockphoto

PRINTING AND PRODUCTION
Catherine Lorrain, Director
Nguyet Tran, Assistant Production Manager

NATIONAL SCIENCE TEACHERS ASSOCIATION
Francis Q. Eberle, PhD, Executive Director
David Beacom, Publisher

LIBRARY OF CONGRESS CATALOGING-IN-PUBLICATION DATA
Glenn, David D.
 Forestry field studies: a manual for science teachers / by David D. Glenn and Donald I. Dickmann.
    p. cm.
  ISBN 978-1-935155-08-9
 1. Forests and forestry—Study and teaching (Secondary)—Activity programs. 2. Forests and forestry—
Study and teaching (Higher)—Activity programs. 3. Forest ecology—Study and teaching (Secondary)—
Activity programs. 4. Forest ecology—Study and teaching (Higher)—Activity programs. 5. Forests and
forestry—Fieldwork. I. Dickmann, Donald I. II. Title.

  SD251.G54 2009

  634.9071—dc22

  eISBN 978-1-936137-98-5   2009030336

NSTA is committed to publishing material that promotes the best in inquiry-based science education. However, conditions of actual use may vary, and the safety procedures and practices described in this book are intended to serve only as a guide. Additional precautionary measures may be required. NSTA and the authors do not warrant or represent that the procedures and practices in this book meet any safety code or standard of federal, state, or local regulations. NSTA and the authors disclaim any liability for personal injury or damage to property arising out of or relating to the use of this book, including any of the recommendations, instructions, or materials contained therein.

CONTENTS

PREFACE

Why forestry field studies? As experienced teachers of scientific ecology and forestry concepts, we believe that a forest or woodlot can provide teachers and their students with the perfect laboratory for understanding some of the basic principles of environmental science and community ecology. These studies were designed and used for many years as a unit in an Advanced Placement environmental science course. They also could be in biology, botany, forestry, or ecology classes at the high school or beginning college levels. The activities place students in a natural environment collecting real data to better understand a real place, something sorely lacking in most high school or beginning college curricula.

Most schools are not very far from a woods of some sort. In certain regions, school districts own their own forests, often underutilized. Some teachers can use a nearby park; others will have the fortune to work in a larger county, state, federal, private, or corporate forest that is within driving distance. To conduct the field activities outlined in this manual, the forest or woodlot could be large or small; deciduous, coniferous, or both; proximal to the school or distant from it. The tree species or forest types available for study are not important; these studies are more about systems and communities than they are about particular trees.

Much research has shown that science instruction and the desired outcome of student understanding are best accomplished by doing in-depth studies on a few concepts, rather than the traditional encyclopedic overview of many subjects. If completed, the field studies presented in this manual represent such an in-depth approach, the goal being a comprehensive examination of a well-defined forest ecosystem. Additionally, these studies represent a valid field experience as defined by the College Board in the course description for Advanced Placement Environmental Science (*http://apcentral.collegeboard.com/apc/public/repository/ap-environmental-science-course-description.pdf*). This description states that field activities should

- always be linked to a major concept in science and to one or more areas of the course outline;

- allow students to have direct experience with an organism or system in the environment;

- involve observation of phenomena or systems, the collection and analysis of data and other information, and the communication of observations and results.

PREFACE

Many of the above ideals of science education are embraced by forestry field studies. Relevant, valid, hands-on work by students collecting real data that they can analyze and interpret is an important aspect of these studies. Just getting students out of the confines of the classroom and into the woods is in itself a worthy effort, let alone having them work on data collection and analysis in a meaningful way. We have noted over the years that the almost universal reaction of students to time spent in the woods is positive; they want to be learning outdoors. For many students this will be a first-time experience; for some it may be a life changing one.

Among the paramount concepts of biology and ecology that can be incorporated into forestry field studies are secondary succession, community structure and function, elemental cycles, population dynamics, biodiversity, global warming, and watershed issues. Additionally, forestry field studies provide the perfect model for introducing the concept of sustainable management of natural resources, which should be part of every student's science education. Working in woodlots provides students with a fixed, workable area in which they can consider important resource management issues such as wildlife habitat, outdoor recreation, biodiversity, and commercial wood production. Because trees are renewable these studies make the concept of sustainability real, relevant, and worthy of consideration. The practical benefit is that students can use their own data to make management recommendations for the forest resource they measured and analyzed. This experience also may open a student's mind to career tracks heretofore not considered.

This manual is organized to take a teacher systematically through a comprehensive set of field exercises, from preparation to written report. We begin by discussing some basic ecology and forestry principles in Chapters 1 and 2. These discussions are meant to be a "refresher course" and do not cover these subjects in a textbook or encyclopedic fashion—for that, see the chapter bibliographies and readings listed in Appendix E. In Chapter 3 we cover some necessary pre-fieldwork preparation. Chapters 4 through 7 describe the actual fieldwork and are essentially units of an all-day session in the woods. If time, budget, or logistics does not permit an all-day field trip, however, one or more units can be chosen to fit a particular situation—we do not intend these exercises to be all or nothing! We conclude with a discussion of the post–field trip data analysis, report writing, and wrap-up.

Spending a day working in the woods doing systematic, observational science using professional tools is just plain fun and exciting, both for students and their teachers. Although the "virtual" experience via some electronic gizmo has become a paradigm of the 21st century, the sights, sounds, smells, and hands-on feeling of a *real* woods have no virtual counterpart. When you and your students experience the woods, you will know what we mean.

ACKNOWLEDGMENTS

This book has been a dream of mine for a very long time. Many people contributed to the science, pedagogy, and logistics of the field studies we describe. First, I'd like to recognize and thank my wife, Sue Ann, for totally supporting this project and for putting up with the incredible amount of time I spent away from home working with students. She also contributed some of the artwork in this book. My colleagues at Rochester Adams High School—especially Scott Short and Joe Wieten—helped me with many of the logistics involved in the field studies. Ned Cavney, retired forester with the Michigan Department of Natural Resources, helped me understand some of the basics of forestry. Bruce Austin, parks and recreation manager for Rochester, Michigan, shared with me his practical experiences in forestry, which helped us develop many of the field studies. Brad Upton, owner of Dillman and Upton lumber company in Rochester, underwrote travel to a workshop to Vancouver, British Columbia, that helped me understand the commercial aspects of forestry. My coauthor has been brilliant on this project and I can't thank him enough. And last, but certainly not least, thanks to all of the hundreds of students I was privileged to work with in the field, doing what foresters, ecologists, and wildlife biologists do.

—*Dave Glenn*

First and foremost, I thank my coauthor for the enthusiasm and passion he brought to this project. I spent a day with him and his students in a woods in Auburn Hills, Michigan, observing them doing the exercises we describe, and this experience cemented my involvement. Those high school kids were doing forestry work, gathering their own data, and loving it! I also would like to thank my friend Bob Crawford for guiding me through the use of his high-resolution slide scanner. Dan Keathley, chair of the Department of Forestry at Michigan State University, provided me with the safe haven of an office, even though I am retired, as well as access to copying and printing equipment. Finally, my wife, Kathleen, gave unqualified and enthusiastic support for this project and always was willing to give advice based on her encyclopedic knowledge of the English language and the publication process.

—*Don Dickmann*

CHAPTER 1
Forest History, Ecology, and Values

Forests have been crucial to human welfare since the dawn of civilization. In ancient times when human populations were small, natural forests supplied wood for fuel, building materials, weapons, and implements in abundance while still protecting the environment. But as human populations grew and their societies became more complex, the exploitation of forests increased. The inevitable consequence was that natural forests were depleted and wood supplies gave out, often with disastrous environmental consequences—destructive floods, wildfires, soil erosion, extinction of species, and pollution. The history of both the Old World and the New World contains many examples of civilizations that failed because they could not sustain their wood supplies and maintain the forest cover that protected and stabilized the environment (Figure 1.1, p. 2). The profession of forestry came into being to remedy this situation.

Figure 1.1. This ancient Anasazi cliff culture in New Mexico failed in part because all the trees in the area were cut down, depleting critical wood supplies.

Figure 1.2. These white pine trees were planted in the 1890s at the Biltmore Estate in Asheville, North Carolina, by America's first college-trained forester, Gifford Pinchot.

Unless otherwise indicated, all photos by D. Dickmann

History of Forestry in the United States

Forestry as a recognized profession did not begin in the United States until the late 1800s, although by that time it was already well established in Europe and parts of Asia. It came about for the usual reasons. Uncontrolled and wasteful logging was cutting more wood than was growing, leaving denuded wastelands behind. Wildfires, often fueled by the debris left after logging, consumed 20 to 50 million acres in the country every year. There was an almost total lack of reforestation of logged and burned lands, while massive tracts of land were cleared for agriculture. And sadly, numerous plant and animal species became extinct or their populations had severely depleted in the process.

Something clearly had to be done. As often is the case, it was the vision of a few people that made the difference. The first native-born American to become a trained forester was Gifford Pinchot. He had to travel to Nancy, France, in 1889 for training because there were no forestry schools in America at that time. Upon returning, Pinchot worked from 1892 to 1895 managing the forests at the huge Biltmore Estate near Asheville, North Carolina. Some of his plantings of white pine can still be seen today at the estate (Figure 1.2). Pinchot was succeeded by a German, Dr. Carl [Schenck,] who formed the Biltmore Forest School in 1898. Because of these historic beginnings, the Biltmore area today is known as the "Cradle of Forestry" in America; it is well worth a visit.

Gifford Pinchot went on to become the first chief of the U.S. Forest Service. He also founded the Society of American Foresters. His boundless energy vitalized these young organizations, and both are still going strong. Pinchot teamed up with President Theodore Roosevelt—one of the leading conservationists of his day—and this dynamic pair greatly enlarged the area of the national forests, especially in the West. But more was needed. College-level education was required to develop a cadre of professional foresters, and it started when Cornell University offered the first forestry curriculum in 1898. Yale followed in 1900 and Michigan Agricultural College (now Michigan State University) in 1902. Soon many more colleges and universities offered forestry as a major. The graduates had plenty to do and they went about it with enthusiasm and determination. Soon destructive logging practices began to be curtailed, logged land was replanted, and fires began to be brought under control. Plants and animals on the verge of extinction started coming back.

From these beginnings the profession of forestry in the United States has grown to the great enterprise it is today, with tens of thousands of foresters and well-managed national, state, county, municipal, reservation, private, or corporate forests in every state. Forestry—which comprises the management of all forest resources, not only timber—is the primary economic engine of many communities, providing jobs and other benefits. Today the area occupied by forests in the United States is estimated to be 72% of what it was in 1630 (prior to European settlement), despite all the clearing that has been done for agriculture, cities and towns, mining, and infrastructure. This area is holding steady at about 750 million acres (Figure 1.3). That is not to say that the forests of today are the same as those of 1630; most old-growth, mature forests, which were cut down or destroyed during more exploitative times, have been replaced by younger, secondary forests or plantations. Especially in the eastern half of the country, forests are fragmented, cut into relatively small blocks bounded by roads and other human developments.

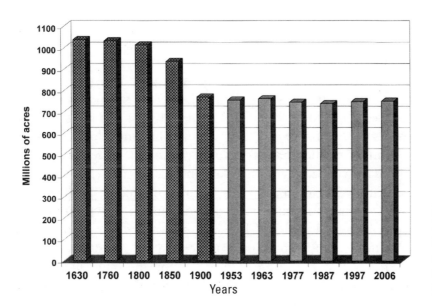

Figure 1.3. Trend in forestland area in the United States from pre-European settlement (1630) to the present. Cross-hatched bars are based on historical evidence; solid bars are based on field sampling by the U.S. Forest Service. (Alvarez 2007).

Figure 1.4. Trees in dry savanna forests—such as these oaks—are scattered or clumped, with prairie or grassland plants growing between them. Savannas are maintained by frequent fires or grazing by ungulates.

Because many of today's secondary forests are becoming more mature, the volume of timber in U.S. forests is growing and exceeds the amount being harvested. This fact bodes well for future supplies of timber products. The forests of today also provide wildlife habitat, watershed protection, carbon sequestration, and a multitude of recreational opportunities. So the vision of Pinchot, Schenck, Roosevelt, and other early foresters paid off—forestry has been a resounding success! But we can't get complacent; forests must continue to be managed wisely or protected to sustain them for future generations.

We also need a continual supply of new foresters and natural resource managers entering the profession. Therefore, an interesting, exciting, and rewarding career track is open to high school students looking toward their future. There currently are 44 accredited undergraduate forestry degree programs offered at universities across the United States (see Appendix A), with numerous schools offering two- and four-year natural resource programs of other kinds. Thus, students with an interest in working in the area of natural resource management have many educational options.

Principles of Forest Ecology

What follows is a discussion of some important ecological concepts. Again, this is just an overview; for detailed coverage of these topics see suggested readings under References in Appendix E.

First of all, what is a forest? Not surprising, a forest is an ecological community whose dominant plants—in size, not number—are trees. But there's more to it than that. A closed forest is what we usually think of—trees are numerous and closely spaced, creating a continuous **overstory** canopy of leaves or needles and deep shade at ground level. In old, mature closed forests, several layers (strata) of trees often grow under the overstory canopy, along with a well-developed **understory** ground flora (see Chapters 4 and 5). Closed forests also are large enough in area to create a distinct environment in the forest interior. An open forest or **savanna** (Figure 1.4), on the other hand, consists of widely spaced or scattered broadleaf or coniferous trees, with a discontinuous canopy that permits lots of sun to reach the ground. In the openings among savanna trees, prairie, grassland, or tundra plants flourish. In many areas today, savannas are much less common than they used to be. The varied and complex community of trees, shrubs, herbs, fungi, animals, and microorganisms that live together in a particular environment constitutes a **forest ecosystem**.

Types of Forests

Forests grow nearly everywhere in the world except in arctic regions, arid plains or steppes, and deserts. They grow on uplands and in wetlands, and they are the most common communities in the terrestrial biosphere. The type of forest ecosystem that exists in a particular area depends principally on temperature, rainfall, and soil properties, although other environmental factors—strong winds, high humidity, fog, and frequent disturbances such as flooding or fires—can be important in some localities. In North America forests are largely temperate or subarctic, although some subtropical forests (e.g., coastal mangroves or sabal palm savannas) occur in south Florida.

North American forests are extremely diverse. **Chaparral** forests, which consist of small broadleaf trees and shrubs, grow in areas where summers are hot and dry and rain falls primarily in the winter, such as in Southern California. Dwarf, savanna-like conifer forests of junipers and pinyon pines (Figure 1.5) occur at lower elevations throughout the Southwest where rainfall is barely enough to support tree growth. Where summers are more cool and moist in western North America, conifer forests consisting mostly of large needle- or cone-bearing trees occur, although some deciduous broadleaf trees that lose their leaves in the winter may commingle with the conifers. The largest trees in the world—redwoods, red cedar, Douglas fir, and Sitka spruce, all conifers—are found along the humid Pacific Coast of North America (Figure 1.6). In eastern North America, where winters are cold, temperate forests largely consisting of deciduous broadleaf trees predominate (Figure 1.7). The diversity of tree species in these forests can be very high. In some northern localities conifers also may be present, and in the South pines are very

Figure 1.5. Distinctive dwarf woodlands of junipers and pinyon pines are found in dry, lower elevations throughout southwestern North America.

Figure 1.6. The largest trees in the world occur in the old-growth conifer forests of the Pacific Coast. This western red cedar behemoth grows in coastal British Columbia.

Figure 1.7. Deciduous broadleaf forests occur in many variants throughout the entire eastern United States.

Figure 1.8. Pine forests, both natural and planted, are a common sight in the southern United States.

common (Figure 1.8). The most northern forests are called **boreal** or **taiga** (Figure 1.9), and they occupy a huge swath of North America. They are largely coniferous, although deciduous trees—principally paper birch and poplars—and many kinds of shrubs also are present.

Rising elevation in high mountains causes a change in climate similar to going north in latitude, and forests change correspondingly. Temperate montane forests are characteristic of midelevations in the mountains (Figure 1.10), and they often are dominated by conifers, especially in the West. Near timberline at high elevations, forests are open and consist principally of stunted conifers and shrubs (Figure 1.11), with tundra plants growing in the open.

Figure 1.9. The taiga or boreal forest occurs throughout the northern latitudes, especially in Canada and Alaska.

Figure 1.10. These Shasta red firs and mountain hemlocks dominate the montane zone at about 6,000 feet elevation in Crater Lake National Park, Oregon.

Figure 1.11. The harsh environment and short growing season at timberline in the mountains—here in Mount Rainier National Park, Washington—creates an open forest of stunted trees.

Figure 1.12. Wetland forests serve an important ecological function by protecting valuable water resources and creating a unique habitat for plants and animals.

Wetland forests occur in or adjacent to streams, rivers, lakes, or oceans (Figure 1.12). They also can occur anywhere that percolation of water through the soil is impaired. The roots of trees that compose these forests are tolerant of low oxygen conditions in the soil created by stagnant or running water, whether these conditions occur year-round or due to periodic flooding. The mangrove forests that grow on the shore of oceans also are tolerant of high salinity. The most important attribute of wetland forests is their protection of the fragile and often very biologically diverse habitats in which they grow.

Besides natural forests, tree plantations have been established in most parts of the world (Figure 1.13). Trees are planted for wood or other tree products, to ameliorate environmental extremes, to protect watersheds, to sequester carbon, or for aesthetic reasons. Pines, spruces, Douglas fir, and poplars are the most common plantation trees in the temperate regions of North America. Australian eucalypts are frequently planted in warm or subtropical regions such as southern Florida or southern California.

Ecological Processes

The large size and slow growth of trees make forests appear stable and permanent, but they actually are continually changing because of climate shifts and disturbances. Earth's climate is not stable and historically has changed in a cyclical manner. The present **Holocene** geologic age, which began about 10,000 years ago, has a very different climate than the **Pleistocene** ice age that preceded it. Even now we are experiencing a general warming trend in Earth's climate. Forests respond as climate changes, but since the pace of climate change is very slow, these changes in forests are difficult to see or measure. Computer models have been built to predict the effects of global warming on forests, but we will never know for sure what will happen until the changes actually occur.

Natural disturbances—fires, high winds, tornadoes, volcanic eruptions, ice storms, floods, avalanches, and insect and disease infestations—occur regularly. Humans also create disturbances. Disturbances can disrupt forests over thousands of acres, in small patches of less than an acre, and every size in between (Figure 1.14). Most ecologists now believe that all forests are in some stage of recovery from the last disturbance. This recovery process is called **secondary succession**. Forest ecosystems are incredibly vital and wonderfully capable of restoring themselves, but recovery following major disturbances may be slow, sometimes taking centuries. In the process, several distinct forest communities succeed one another.

Figure 1.13. Tree plantations are a common sight in many parts of North America. This one is an eastern conifer—red pine—and it has recently been thinned by removing every third row.

Figure 1.14. Disturbances are common occurrences in forests, and they range in scale from very small (wind breakage of a few trees—above) to very large (the aftermath of a severe wildfire—below). Secondary succession follows a disturbance.

Figure 1.15. Intolerant, pioneer trees—like these young aspen sprouts—are among the first plants to establish following a major disturbance, beginning the process of secondary succession.

Figure 1.16. Sometimes pioneer trees that reestablish following a large natural disturbance can form extensive even-aged monocultures. Here lodgepole pine has returned following the 1988 wildfires in Yellowstone National Park. Photo courtesy of Paul Bolstad, University of Minnesota, *www.Bugwood.org*

The trees that form early successional forests immediately following a disturbance are called **intolerant pioneers** (Figure 1.15). They adapt to resource-rich environments and grow best in full sunlight. Therefore they are referred to as being intolerant of the shaded conditions under an established forest. Examples are quaking aspen, paper and gray birch, tulip poplar, sweet gum, most pine species, red alder, and larches (see Appendix D). Early successional forests usually are **even-aged** (i.e., all the trees are more or less the same age) because they became established together, although some older trees may have survived the disturbance. These successional forests sometimes are single-tree monocultures (Figures 1.15 and 1.16), and if the disturbance is extensive, they can occupy thousands of acres. As time goes on during secondary succession, the total living biomass (weight) of organisms in a forest community and their diversity slowly rises because critical resources—space, light, water, and nutrients—are plentiful. During this aggregation phase total community photosynthesis exceeds respiration, and there is a net release of oxygen into the atmosphere.

Eventually a more-or-less stable living biomass is reached that usually is maintained until the next disturbance occurs. Total community photosynthesis and respiration during this mature phase are approximately equal. The structure of the forest becomes more complex during the mature phase as young tree species that are tolerant of shade (spruces, firs, hemlocks, black tupelo, beech, dogwood, and sugar maple [see Appendix D]) become established under the older trees, creating a diverse, **uneven-aged** forest (Figure 1.17). Eventually—barring another disturbance—the forest reaches an old-growth phase, where tolerant species and residual intolerant species that can live a long time dominate (Figures 1.6 and 1.10). The tolerant late successional species can survive and reproduce themselves in full or partial shade and can successfully compete in soils full of tree roots. In the old-growth phase total community living biomass actually may decline, and total respiration may exceed photosynthesis, as large trees of great weight die and decay.

The members of forest communities interact with one another in complex ways. Competition for available resources in the soil and air—water, mineral nutrients, oxygen, carbon dioxide, sunlight, food, and space—is intense. Demand exceeds supply, so organisms continually die from want. Others are victims of disease, animal or insect grazing, or predation. In a process called **mutualism**, organisms interact with others in beneficial ways. For example, insects get nectar from flowers in the act of pollinating them; bacteria and fungi decompose organic matter to get food, in the process releasing essential mineral nutrients that other organisms can use (Figure 1.18). In one of the most fascinating and widespread examples of mutualism, tree roots are invaded by the hyphae of mycorrhizal fungi; the fungi get carbohydrates from the tree roots and in turn aid the roots in extracting nutrients from the soil.

Established forests are "tight" ecosystems; mineral nutrients are recycled efficiently and few leach into ground water, escape in stream outflow and erosion, or are lost to the atmosphere. When nutrients are released into the soil through decay (**mineralization**), they are immediately snatched up by roots and microorganisms. In certain tropical forests, soils are rather sterile, and virtually all of the nutrients are bound up in living and dead organisms. Major disturbances disrupt tight nutrient cycling, and until a new early successional community is well established, nutrients move downslope or downstream and the system becomes temporarily "leaky."

Figure 1.17. Eventually short-lived pioneer trees are replaced by tolerant, late successional trees, creating a more complex, diverse, uneven-aged structure, like the spruce-fir-cedar stand shown here.

Forest Values

Forests are the most important natural communities on Earth for people, and they have been used since the dawn of time. The value of various forest uses is incalculable, and life as we know it would be impossible without forests. Some uses are **consumptive**; that is, a commodity or product is extracted from the forest. Other uses are **non-consumptive**. A benefit, service, or value is provided by a forest simply being there and functioning as an intact ecosystem.

The most widely used consumptive forest product is wood. Consumption of wood products in the United States is just under three-quarters of a ton per person per year! Wood also is the world's most versatile raw material because of its unique physical, mechanical, and chemical properties; because the wood from

Figure 1.18. In a forest, death is as important as life because the nutrients in decaying organisms are released back into the soil where living organisms can use them. This dead log also provides a habitat for certain animals and insects.

Figure 1.19. Sawn lumber still is a very important forest product. It is used in construction and to make many secondary products such as furniture, paneling, cabinets, or the flooring shown here.
Photo courtesy of John Yarema.

Figure 1.20. Oriented strand board (OSB), a common construction material, can be made by chipping small trees that otherwise have few uses.

the multitude of tree species is extremely diverse; and because wood is relatively inexpensive and widely available. In the wood products business trees are divided into two categories based on their wood structure, properties, and uses. Coniferous, needle-bearing trees like pines, spruces, hemlocks, and firs are called **softwoods**, whereas broadleaf trees like oaks, maples, ashes, alder, and poplars are called **hardwoods**.

Products made from solid wood have been used since humans' earliest days, but they are by no means obsolete (Figure 1.19). Sawn lumber and timbers (boards like 2 × 4s, 2 × 6s, and 4 × 4s) still are widely used for construction and for manufacturing of all kinds of secondary products—furniture, cabinets, doors, flooring, and interior trim. Lumber also can be glue-laminated into beams or, if used outside, treated with chemicals to prevent decay. Softwood lumber is primarily used for construction, whereas hardwoods are favored for furniture and interior decorative uses. Plywood is another important solid wood product that is made by peeling or slicing wood from logs, creating plies. The plies are then glued together so that the grain crosses to give strength. Plywood is used for construction and for various secondary products such as furniture or cabinets. Solid wood also is used for utility poles, posts, pilings, cabin logs, bentwood furniture, and a host of other uses.

Wood from small trees can be chipped or flaked and then manufactured into composite boards—such as oriented strand board or OSB (Figure 1.20). Composites are used in construction, the core of plywood, and ceiling tile, among other uses. Wood-plastic composite boards are a new technology that is becoming more common, especially for exterior uses. The projected rise in wood use in the United States in the next 50 years will be primarily in the form of these composite products.

Paper was first made from pulped wood fibers about 150 years ago. Pulping involves the treatment of wood chips with chemicals, dissolving the lignin that glues wood together and releasing the cellulose fibers. Most paper today still is made from wood, both softwoods and hardwoods. Besides paper, wood's cellulose fibers and the other chemical constituents of pulp are manufactured into a wide array of products such as cardboard, rayon, lacquers, plastics, turpentine, medicines, and methanol.

As the price of oil continues to rise, wood increasingly will be used for energy, in solid wood form or converted to a liquid biofuel such as ethanol.

Other consumptive forest products are not wood-based. Syrup and sugar have long been made by boiling the sap from maple trees—primarily sugar maple—in early spring (Figure 1.21). Harvesting game animals for food, fur, or feathers has a long history that parallels that of humans and still is an important activity for many people. Grazing by domestic livestock occurs in certain forests, and in some countries tree leaves are fed to livestock. Trees and forests provide nuts, fruit, mushrooms, medicines, greenery, and Christmas trees. Watersheds—many of which are forested—comprise all of the land that drains to a particular body of water. Some of them are managed strictly to protect municipal water supplies.

Nonconsumptive uses of forests are very important too. Outdoor recreation activities (see Chapter 7)—such as camping, hiking, skiing, riding horses or off-road vehicles, wildlife watching, and photography—are extremely important in contemporary society. For some people forests provide a place of solace, even a spiritual experience (Figure 1.22). Forests also provide many ecosystem services by maintaining and improving the environment, preventing erosion and flooding, and purifying air and water by filtering out pollutants.

The concentrations of carbon dioxide (CO_2) and other greenhouse gases (GHG) in the atmosphere have been rising since about 1750 (pre–Industrial Revolution). Based on observed increases in average global air and ocean temperatures, widespread melting of snow and ice, and rising average sea level, the global climate is unequivocally warming. According to the International Panel on Climate Change (Bernstein et al. 2007), "Most of the observed increase in global average temperatures since the mid-20th century is very likely due to the observed increase in anthropogenic GHG concentrations."

Forests are considered to be a major carbon sink—they take CO_2 from the air through photosynthesis and convert it to biomass, slowing the buildup of CO_2 and moderating climate change. This process of **carbon sequestration** is becoming recognized as a major nonconsumptive benefit of forests (Figure

Figure 1.21. In northeastern North America, where sugar maple grows, the production of maple syrup is a very important and colorful local industry.

Figure 1.22. In the quiet of a forest, many people find solace and spiritual refreshment or a welcome respite from the frantic pace of modern life.

Figure 1.23. According to data from the U.S. Environmental Protection Agency (EPA 2009), in 2007 forests in the U.S. sequestered 910.1 million metric tons of CO_2, which represents an offset of 14.9% of total American CO_2 emissions that year.

1.23, p. 11). As a result, trading of carbon sequestration credits (cap and trade) now occurs on the Chicago Climate Exchange. If we are to make any progress in curbing rising CO_2 levels, we must avoid deforestation, whether it involves clearing of large tracts of forest for strip mining, agriculture, or any other reason or bulldozing woodlots and paving them with asphalt for shopping malls and other developments.

References

Aber, J. D., and J. M. Melillo. 2002. *Terrestrial ecosystems.* 2nd ed. Florence, KY: Brooks/Cole.

Alvarez, M. 2007. *The state of America's forests.* Bethesda, MD: Society of American Foresters *(www.safnet.org/aboutforestry/StateOfAmericasForests.pdf)*.

Bailey, R. G. 1995. *Descriptions of the ecoregions of the United States.* Washington, DC: USDA Forest Service. Miscellaneous Publication No. 1391.

Barnes, B. V., D. R. Zak, S. R. Denton, and S. H. Spurr. 1998. *Forest ecology.* 4th ed. New York: John Wiley & Sons.

Bernstein, L., P. Bosch, O. Canziani, Z. Chen, R. Christ, O. Davidson, W. Hare, et al. 2007. *Climate change 2007: Synthesis report.* Summary for policy makers. Intergovernmental Panel on Climate Change *(www.ipcc.ch/pdf/assessment-report/ar4/syr/ar4_syr_spm.pdf)*.

Burns, R. M., and B. H. Honkala. 1965. *Silvics of North America.* USDA Forest Service Agriculture Handbook 654 *(www.na.fs.fed.us/spfo/pubs/silvics_manual/table_of_contents.htm)*.

EPA. 2009. *Inventory of U.S. greenhouse gas emissions and sinks: 1990–2007.* Washington, DC: U.S. Environmental Protection Agency 430-R-09-004 *(http://epa.gov/climatechange/emissions/usinventoryreport.html)*.

Walker, L. C. 1997. *Forests: A naturalist's guide to woodland trees.* Austin: University of Texas Press.

CHAPTER 2
Principles of Forestry

The core value of forestry is the long-term sustainability of forests. Sustainability can be accomplished only if we understand ecological processes and respect them; then we can creatively protect and shape forests to satisfy the needs of future generations. In the early days of American forestry, a primary duty of foresters was to protect against destructive disturbances, particularly forest fires, insect outbreaks, and disease infestations. Reforestation of disturbed areas also was a high priority. While protection and reforestation are still major activities of foresters, the field has become much more wide-ranging and diversified as landowner objectives have broadened, society has demanded more input into forest management, budgetary limitations and other economic concerns have increased, and technologies have become more complex and sophisticated.

Figure 2.1. *Ecosystem management* calls for planning over a long time frame with entire landscapes in mind, rather than focusing on just a few trees or stands.

Figure 2.2. Wildfires are a constant threat to forests across North America, and many of them—like this firestorm—are impossible to put out unless the weather changes.

Unless otherwise indicated, all photos by D. Dickmann.

The overarching paradigm that guides management by many large landowners today is called **ecosystem management.** This paradigm states that no one commodity or use is more important than any other, so the objective of management should be to maintain the vitality of ecosystems, including all the organisms in them. If this is done, then commodities that people want—like timber or game—can be taken from the forest but other noncommodity values will not be diminished. Management under this principle also encompasses all the ecosystems in a large landscape area, not just a few that we think are most important (Figure 2.1). Finally, ecosystem management takes the long-term view; the one-year or five-year plan just will not do. The plan must result from thinking decades or even centuries into the future and allow for changing ownership priorities, new laws, expanding knowledge, and the likelihood of unwanted natural disturbances.

The need for ecologically, economically, and socially sustainable forest management has led to formal forest certification programs in the United States and worldwide. To become a certified forest, property and its personnel are evaluated by an independent third party who determines if that property meets a well-defined set of management standards. If met, the property is certified, usually for a period of five years. Products from that property then can be labeled as certified so potential buyers can be assured that they came from a sustainably managed forest. The Forest Stewardship Council and the Sustainable Forestry Initiative are the major certifying organizations in the United States and Canada. Certified properties currently include tree farms, industrial forests, timber investment organizations, tribal lands, and state, county, and university forests.

Dealing With Disturbances

The regular yet largely unpredictable occurrence of natural disturbances can completely derail the most carefully prepared long-range management plan. **Wildfires** in forests and other wildlands still are a major problem plaguing foresters and other resource managers (Figure 2.2). During the period from 1999 to 2008, 799,000 wildfires burned more than 69 million acres (108,000 square miles!) in the United States [(data from the National Interagency Fire Center, *www.nifc.gov*).] These fires not only destroyed valuable timber and other natural resources and set back ecological succession, but because many people live or recreate in forested areas, thousands of homes, vacation structures, and other buildings were consumed. Tragically, some human and countless animal lives also were lost. In some areas of the country—California, much of the Rocky Mountain West, Texas, and the Deep South—firefighting budgets and resources are severely strained, yet this problem shows no signs of abating.

Massive insect outbreaks on a heretofore unheard-of scale also have recently complicated forest management, calling for the implementation of contingency plans. In many parts of western North America decadelong drought conditions have put trees under stress, while rising temperatures and longer growing seasons have produced additional insect generations. As a result, millions of acres of aging pine and spruce forests have been devastated by bark beetles (Figure 2.3). Meanwhile in the East, exotic invasive insects that have few or no natural controls—gypsy moth, emerald ash borer, hemlock wooly adelgid, and beech scale (which transmits beech bark disease)—have devastated many millions of trees and put the continued existence of some of the host trees in doubt. With global temperatures continuing to rise and more exotic insects slipping unnoticed into North America, we can expect more havoc to occur.

The frustration faced by foresters comes from knowing full well that natural disturbances—often catastrophic and from unexpected quarters—will occur, but that they have little control over them. And even if prevention or suppression of disturbances are possible, the costs usually are prohibitive. So foresters must concentrate on what they can do in an ecologically appropriate, cost-efficient, and socially acceptable manner to manage their forests, while glancing over their shoulders for the inevitable, plan-upsetting wildfire, insect outbreak, or other disturbance. A big part of forest management is silviculture.

Figure 2.3. Epidemic insect outbreaks have exacted a huge toll from North American forests in past decades, with no end in sight. The light-hued ponderosa pine trees in this photo from the Black Hills of South Dakota were killed by the mountain pine beetle. Photo courtesy of USDA Forest Service-Rocky Mountain Region Archive, *www.Bugwood.org*.

Figure 2.4. This couple enjoys the many benefits that their *tree farm* provides, including income from harvests of timber.
Photo courtesy of the Michigan Tree Farm System.

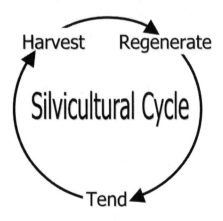

Figure 2.5. The *silvicultural cycle*. The distance around the cycle represents time in the life of a stand.

Silvicultural Methods

Silviculture[1] is the practice of establishing or shaping the kind of forest that best fits the objectives of the landowner. It is the foundation of scientific management of forest ecosystems. Just like the growing of a field of corn, wheat, or peanuts is agriculture, the purposeful growing of a forest for consumptive or nonconsumptive human benefits—be it a plantation or a natural forest—is silviculture. Professional foresters usually are the practitioners of silviculture, but anyone who owns a forest can do silviculture, provided they are willing to learn something about forest ecology and silvicultural methods first.

The practice of silviculture must be very adaptable because the ecology of each kind of forest is different, plus the diverse owners of forests want different things from them. For example, many private landowners desire a place to enjoy nature's beauty, find solace, and watch wildlife. Other owners, like a land conservancy or a conservation district, want to protect water sources, maintain or increase biodiversity, or preserve a rare or endangered plant, animal, or ecosystem. These intangible or noncommodity benefits are very important to many people. Still other owners—tree farmers or forest products companies—want their forests to produce commodities such as timber, pulpwood, fuelwood, game, mushrooms, or something else they can sell (Figure 2.4). Forests owned by public agencies (e.g., national, state, county, municipal, or tribal forests) typically are mandated to provide both noncommodity and commodity benefits; their management is oriented to multiple uses. So before anyone practices silviculture they must have clearly in mind what the landowner wants from the forest (i.e., owner's objectives).

In general, silvicultural methods are applied at three stages in the life of a forest: (1) the tending stage, when established trees in a forest are growing and maturing; (2) the reproductive or regeneration stage, when a forest—or some part of it—is becoming established from seedlings or sprouts; and (3) the harvest stage, when some or all fully mature trees are harvested and utilized (Figure 2.5). The tending stage lasts the longest, while the reproductive stage immediately follows a disturbance or harvest.

---

[1]See Appendix B-1 for a glossary of ecological and forestry terms commonly used in silviculture.

The latter may be optional. For example, if a landowner wants an old-growth forest and is not interested in selling timber, they may choose not to harvest any old, mature trees. So the tending stage just continues.

Some silvicultural treatments involve **logging**, or cutting down trees (Figure 2.6). Logging often involves the use of powerful, sophisticated, and expensive equipment, but in ecologically sensitive areas chain saws and a team of horses still may be all that are used. Although foresters are not loggers, they use logging to carry out their silvicultural plans for a forest. People can get upset about logging because the lives of large trees are terminated, the process creates ugliness, and they feel it harms the environment. But logging is a necessary part of silviculture, and the wood it supplies is essential to maintaining the standard of living we all want and enjoy. If done correctly by caring, knowledgeable loggers, the negative effects of tree harvesting are minimal and nature quickly heals the logged area. In many cases loggers are required to follow Best Management Practices (BMP), which have been formulated on a state-by-state basis to protect water, soil, and the environment. As in any profession there are incompetent or unscrupulous loggers, but most are honest and want to do the right thing.

We'll discuss briefly some of the treatments that can be done during each of the three stages of silviculture. The best way to understand these treatments is to visualize a forest or tract of land with which you are familiar, then imagine a given treatment being applied to it. Or better still, get out on a nice day and do the exercises outlined in this manual. The data you and your students collect will give important clues as to what might be the appropriate silviculture to apply to accomplish a given set of objectives.

Figure 2.6. Foresters use *logging* to accomplish many silvicultural objectives. If done properly, logging is not harmful to forests.

Tending Treatments

Release
Release usually is the first tending treatment done in a regenerating forest. This treatment involves freeing seedling or sapling trees from competition by undesirable weeds, shrubs, other young but undesirable trees, or old trees that are shading

or suppressing them (Figure 2.7). Release usually is accomplished by cutting the weedy plants or spraying them with herbicides.

Figure 2.7. These young loblolly pines in Alabama will survive and grow better if they are *released* from the weeds engulfing them by mowing or spraying with a herbicide.

Thinning

Thinning is a common tending treatment carried out in well-established, even-aged forests. It is a way to alter competition by taking out the weaker (smaller) trees so that the stronger (larger) trees can get more resources and grow faster (Figure 2.8). Thinning also can remove tree species that are of less value or trees that are crooked, broken-off, or rotten. In most cases one-third to half of the trees in a forest are removed in a thinning. In plantations whole rows of trees often are cut (see Figure 1.13, p. 7), which is a very efficient way to do a thinning. Again, if you walk through or measure the density a crowded forest or a plantation (see Chapter 5) you can readily envision how it could be thinned. Trees removed in thinning usually can be sold by the landowner for lumber, pulpwood, or posts or can be cut up for firewood.

Figure 2.8. A sugar maple stand in Michigan that was *thinned* by harvesting about one-third of the trees. The harvested logs provided income for the landowner while the growth rate of the remaining trees increased.

Pruning

Pruning removes all of the dead and some live branches on the lower trunks of trees and often is done immediately following thinning. Trees that are pruned produce knot-free (clear) wood that is much higher in value than knotty wood. Pruning also can be done to improve safety and facilitate access and for aesthetic reasons. Branches should be sawed or clipped off flush with the stem or the swelling at the base of the branch, leaving no stubs (Figure 2.9).

Figure 2.9. This young oak tree was *pruned* properly by sawing off the branches flush with the stem. Note how the pruning wound has healed over.

Prescribed Burning

Many ecologists and foresters believe that catastrophic wildfires in recent years are due, ironically, to the exclusion of fire by active fire prevention and suppression programs. Small, low-intensity fires (Figure 2.10) actually are beneficial to many forests, and they can prevent a conflagration from occurring by consuming fuels that have built up. Even Smokey the Bear has become wise to this principle; his message has changed from "Only you can prevent *forest* fires" to "Only you can prevent *wildfires.*" The implication is obvious—not all fires in the woods are bad; hence the need for prescribed burning. Although fire is a potentially dangerous tool, prescribed fire can accomplish several goals. Besides reducing hazardous fuel buildup, these fires can also

- control undesirable small trees and shrubs in the understory while favoring fire-adapted herbs and tree species;
- increase biodiversity;
- improve wildlife habitat;
- control certain harmful diseases and insects; and
- create more open, accessible conditions.

Figure 2.10. A low intensity *prescribed burn* in a pine stand. If done properly, these fires consume dangerous fuels and produce beneficial changes in the understory without harming the large overstory trees.

Although prescribed burning can do much good, it should be done *only* by trained, experienced people guided by a deliberate, written plan. Most of these fires are set purposefully, but sometimes a fire ignited by lightning will be allowed to burn if conditions are right. Prescribed burning should be employed in forests that are naturally adapted to fires, such as those composed primarily of pines, other thick-barked conifers, or oaks.

Natural Reproduction Methods

These silvicultural methods, which follow the tending stage, are based on some form of timber harvest (logging). They stimulate reproduction of young trees in a forest by creating a disturbance. The natural process of secondary succession then takes over after the logging is done. Thus, these methods rely on the unstoppable reproductive force in nature. The natural tree reproduction that takes hold in a harvested area can come from a number of sources:

- Seed blown in or carried in by animals from adjacent, undisturbed stands
- Seed from trees intentionally left standing in the harvested area
- Seed from harvested trees that had already fallen to the ground
- Seed released from cones or fruits in the tops of harvested trees that are left behind

Figure 2.11. A young hardwood-pine forest in northern Georgia that grew back after a *silvicultural clear-cut* about 10 years earlier. Note the uncut forest in the background.

- Seed that has lain dormant in the forest floor for many years
- Tolerant seedlings or saplings that were already growing in the understory of the harvested stand
- Sprouts from the stumps or roots of trees that were cut down

Natural reproduction methods traditionally have been divided into four categories: **clear-cutting**, **seed tree**, **shelterwood**, and **selection**. Each can be used in several different ways and they overlap one another. To create more diversity, several methods can be combined over a large area. The most important point about natural reproduction is to let the ecology of the forest being cut tell you what is the best method or methods to use.

Clear-cutting

This method is widely used but highly controversial. It involves cutting all or virtually all trees in a defined area. Clear-cutting is like a severe natural disturbance such as a fire, tornado, volcanic eruption, or deadly insect outbreak that destroys a whole forest. Unfortunately, the results are not pretty. But natural succession in a clear-cut area is really no different than what happens after a natural disturbance. Thus, silvicultural clear-cutting does not destroy forests; rather, it resets the successional clock. Human development—cities, subdivisions, malls, roads, airports, agricultural fields, strip mining, and so on—is what destroys forests. Nature, however, is not always in a hurry—as we seem to be—so a new forest may take some time to regenerate after clear-cutting. In other cases the forest returns almost immediately following harvesting (Figure 2.11). Virtually all forests in America east of the Mississippi River, as well as many western forests, were clear-cut in the past, in some areas several times. Yet the area of forestland in the United States during the past 100 years has stayed relatively constant (Figure 1.3, p. 3), testifying that forests do come back following clear-cutting.

Clear-cutting can be used in virtually any kind of forest, but if the forest is very old and uneven-aged, other methods (see below) may be better. In the past clear-cutting was done in old-growth forests, but what remains of these forests should be protected, not harvested. Clear-cuts vary in size from a few acres to a few thousand acres. Although many people prefer small clear-cuts, large clear-cuts can be beneficial because they mimic large-scale natural disturbances, reduce landscape fragmentation, and create habitats on a scale required by certain animals. For example, Michigan's endangered Kirtland's warbler requires large tracts of young, regenerating jack pines. On the other hand, the mature-forest habitat of deep-woods animals such as the northern spotted owl or the pine marten are destroyed by clear-cutting; no one silvicultural practice can benefit all wildlife species.

Under ecosystem management some trees may be left standing in a "clear-cut," either alone, in small groups, or in islands up to several acres in size (Figure 2.12). These retained trees make a large opening look better and provide habitat for certain birds, animals, and other creatures. Today the borders of clear-cuts tend to be irregular, as opposed to the square or rectangular openings so prevalent in earlier times. Irregular boundaries are similar to those found around natural disturbances, create more "edge" for wildlife, and look better.

Figure 2.12. This *retention "clear-cut"* in Michigan left some large white pine trees behind to provide seed, soften the look of the area, and maintain ecosystem diversity.

Seed tree

This method is not that different from an ecosystem management clear-cut, except that trees (usually 5 to 20 per acre) are left standing expressly to provide seed to regenerate the harvested area. The seed-tree method should not be used where the soil is shallow or excessively wet, because most of the shallow-rooted seed trees will blow over. Nonetheless, some loss of trees from wind breakage, uprooting by the wind, or other natural causes will inevitably occur.

Shelterwood

This partial-cutting method typically leaves one-third to half of the mature, overstory trees standing, alone or in groups (Figure 2.13). The trees that are left provide seed to regenerate the forest and shelter to lessen harsh environmental conditions (see Chapter 5). Under a shelterwood, the ground at any spot will be shaded at least some time during the course of hot, sunny days,

Figure 2.13. This Douglas fir stand in western Washington was recently harvested using the *shelterwood system.* The large trees left behind provide both a source of seed and light shade for young seedlings.

Figure 2.14. *Uneven-aged forests*—like this ponderosa pine stand in Arizona—can be managed using the selection system. Scattered individual trees or small groups of trees are cut creating openings in which young trees can regenerate.

and the overstory trees provide protection from late-spring and early fall frosts. Shelterwood is the most versatile of all natural reproduction methods; conditions can be adjusted to favor reproduction of virtually any tree species, whether tolerant or intolerant (see Appendix D). When young trees become established, but usually before they reach the sapling stage, some or all of the overstory trees can be removed in a second logging. If the residual overstory is not cut, then the resulting stand becomes two-storied or stratified. A big advantage of shelterwood is that after the first harvest, a forest is left behind that still looks good, although much thinned out.

Selection

This method removes scattered mature trees alone or in small groups in an uneven-aged stand, producing a number of small gaps or patches. Selection was designed to imitate the kind of disturbance that occurs when wind uproots or snaps off a single large tree (see Figure 1.14, p. 7), which in turn sometimes brings a few other trees down with it. If you walk through any old, mature forest you will see that trees are being blown down all the time, creating gaps in the overhead leaf canopy. No more than one-fifth of the trees in a stand are removed at any one time in a selection harvest (often less), and the basic structure and environment of the stand are not changed in a significant way. A cycle is established for a stand in which in 5 to 15 years later another selection harvest can be carried out, and so on into the future. If done correctly, periodic selection cutting can go on indefinitely, leaving the forest mostly intact (Figure 2.14). Reproduction in small gaps, however, will occur for largely tolerant tree species like sugar maple, hemlocks, firs, or spruces.

If more intolerant trees—pines, Douglas fir, or oaks—are wanted, then the post-harvest gaps should be larger, sometimes up to one-half acre in size. If these larger gaps are used the method is called **group selection**, because a number of trees in a group are harvested at one time. Because the overall structure of the forest is only altered slightly, the selection method looks good and maintains the habitat required by deep-woods animals such as the wood thrush, northern spotted owl, or pine marten.

Planting

Planting is done in places where natural reproduction cannot be counted on to reforest a large disturbed area quickly (e.g., clear-cut, wildfire, volcanic eruption), when open land is reforested, or when the landowner wants the type of forest to be changed. In the latter case, the change usually has been from a hardwood forest to a conifer plantation. Planting is the most reliable form of forest regeneration, and the choice of tree species is yours. But planting is expensive, and if it is not done right, it can fail.

Plantations mostly are monocultures—they consist of a single tree species. Monocultures are viewed negatively by many people, yet they are common in nature and by no means unique to plantations. For example, one can drive for miles through natural monocultures of ponderosa pine in the Southwest (Figure 2.14) and lodgepole pine in the Rocky Mountains (Figure 1.16, p. 8). Single-species plantations are the norm because they are easier to manage and more productive (Figure 2.15). The most frequently planted trees in the United States are conifers, mostly pines and Douglas fir, with some spruces and firs also planted, the latter mostly for Christmas trees. By the year 2050 about 60% of the conifer harvest from private lands in America will come from plantations, showing the importance of this form of silviculture. Black walnut, oaks, sweet gum, sycamore, and poplars are the most commonly planted hardwoods, but their total acreage is far less than the conifers. Most of the commonly planted tree species have been genetically improved; they have been specially bred to have better growth, disease resistance, and wood properties. However, no bioengineered trees (also called **genetically modified organisms** or GMO) have been planted on a large scale or for commercial purposes, although several are being tested under the tightly controlled conditions mandated by the U.S. Department of Agriculture and the Environmental Protection Agency.

Trees usually are planted as bare-root seedlings (Figure 2.16). Seed is sowed in a nursery and the seedlings are grown for one to four years before the roots are lifted out of the ground. After they are packaged, lifted seedlings are stored in a large refrigerator before they are taken to the planting site. If the seedlings are carefully planted in the soil and cool, rainy weather follows, most

Figure 2.15. Most *tree plantations*—this one loblolly pine on industrial land in South Carolina—are monocultures. What they lack in biodiversity they make up for in high wood production.

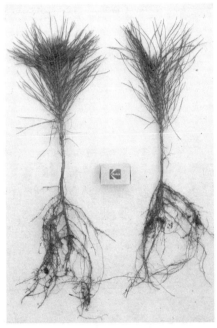

Figure 2.16. *Bare-root seedlings* grown in a nursery are widely used to establish tree plantations for wood products, Christmas trees, and other benefits.

of the young trees will survive and grow. But hot, dry weather can be deadly to recently planted seedlings. That is why most tree planting is done in the early spring, fall, or—in the South and low-elevation Pacific Northwest—winter.

Sometimes tree seedlings are grown in small pots or containers, then removed from the containers and planted. This practice can improve seedling survival in marginal weather or soil conditions. Willows and certain poplars are planted using cuttings, which are short (10–20 inch) lengths of one-year-old stems that are stuck into the ground. Plantations established from cuttings are clonal; all the resultant trees have the same genetic makeup. In the future advances in biotechnology will enable many other tree species to be planted in clonal plantations, improving productivity.

Applications of Silviculture

Because the silvicultural plan for any forest depends on both the ecology of that particular forest and the landowner's objectives, there is wide variation across the United States in the way silviculture is practiced. Because forests across the length and breadth of the country are so different, their silviculture is correspondingly different. Although the same basic methods discussed above are used everywhere, the frequency of their use and the fine points of their application vary regionally. Just one example will illustrate this point. In Deep South states such as Georgia, North and South Carolina, Alabama, and Mississippi, the most important native pine—loblolly—is managed principally in plantations of genetically improved trees harvested after 25 years or less (Figure 2.15). In fact, more trees—and they are mostly loblolly pine—are planted in the South than in any other part of the country. In contrast, the native ponderosa pine of the Southwest and Rocky Mountains is planted infrequently. Most of the management of ponderosa employs natural reproduction systems like selection, and trees may be grown for more than 100 years before they are harvested (Figure 2.14, p. 22).

Ownership objectives also cause wide variation in silviculture. On the one hand, owners of natural tracts of forestland who want a wide range of benefits from them and who value wildness and

Figure 2.17. Landowners who prefer a "light touch" practice *extensive silviculture,* which ensures that timber harvesting will cause minimum disruption of their forests.

stability usually practice extensive silviculture (Figure 2.17). In the most extreme case, silviculturists would do nothing, but this is not a very challenging situation for a silviculturist! In a slightly more intensive case they would harvest trees infrequently and rely strictly on natural reproduction. Rarely would they use clear-cutting, but rather they would employ a shelterwood or selection system. Tending methods would not be used very often. These owners' major objective is to let natural ecological processes prevail, with minor inputs of silviculture and minimum outputs of consumptive products. To say it another way, practitioners of extensive silviculture let the forest lead the forester.

On the other hand are landowners, such as large forest products companies or tree farmers, who want their forests to produce the maximum amount of timber, pulpwood, or some other consumptive product in the shortest amount of time. They practice intensive silviculture in plantations of genetically improved "super trees" created by selective breeding (Figure 2.18). They might use all or most of the tending practices discussed, some several times. When the plantations reach harvest age they are clear-cut, the site is intensively prepared, and a new plantation is established with the latest generation of super trees. Silviculture of this intensity can be more like agriculture than forestry. In this case, we can say that the forester leads the forest.

Of course, there are many landowners who practice a form of silviculture that is somewhere between highly extensive and highly intensive. There's plenty of room in this middle ground to accommodate most landowners. Regardless of how silviculture is practiced, the watchword is *sustainability*. The worst thing is to mismanage a forest to the point that its trees are destroyed and its ecological processes and environment degraded. Sadly, this happens all too often when people exploit a forest only for the money it can return—either willfully or through ignorance—with no thought for the future. But the careful and creative application of silviculture prevents this from happening, allowing landowners and their descendants to enjoy the benefits that forests provide long into the future.

With this background in mind, you and your students now are ready to visit a forest in your locality; measure its ecological, environmental, and commercial properties; and then develop a

Figure 2.18. This hybrid poplar tree farm in the state of Washington exemplifies *intensive silviculture,* which is more like agriculture than forestry and produces a high yield of wood products.

silvicultural management plan. We think you will find it great fun as well as a meaningful learning experience. The following chapters will tell you exactly how to proceed.

References

Food and Agriculture Organization of the United Nations (FAO). 2009. *State of the world's forests: 2009*. Rome: Electronic Publishing Policy and Support Branch, FAO (*www.fao.org/forestry/sofo/en*).

Ford-Roberston, F. C., and R. K. Winters, eds. 1983. *Terminology of forest science technology practice and products*. Washington, DC: Society of American Foresters.

Haynes, R. W. 2003. *An analysis of the timber situation in the United States: 1952 to 2050*. Portland, OR: U.S. Department of Agriculture, Forest Service, Pacific Northwest Research Station (*www.treesearch.fs.fed.us/pubs/5284*).

MacCleery, D. W. 1994. *American forests: A history of resiliency and recovery*, 3rd ed. Durham, NC: Forest History Society.

McEvoy, T. J. 2004. *Positive impact forestry*. Washington, DC: Island Press.

Morsbach, H. 2004. *Common sense forestry*. White River Junction, VT: Chelsea Green Publishing.

Nyland, R. D. 2002. *Silviculture: Concepts and applications*. 2nd ed. New York: McGraw-Hill.

Oliver, C. D., and B. C. Larson. 1996. *Forest stand dynamics*. Update ed. New York: John Wiley & Sons.

Young, R. A., and R. L. Giese, eds. 2003. *Introduction to forest ecosystem science and management*. 3rd ed. New York: John Wiley & Sons.

CHAPTER 3
Setting the Stage

Unquestionably, conducting successful field studies with high school or beginning college students is complicated, energy consuming, and challenging. Nonetheless, putting students in the field to collect real data, analyze the data, and eventually draw conclusions from the data to create a resource management plan makes it all worthwhile. There is more to forests than the trees—as important as they are—and the exercises we discuss can give students a glimpse into not only the complexity and biological diversity of forests but also their economic value.

In this chapter we frame some of the activities and planning that go into producing a relevant, rewarding, and fun experience for students. These ideas have been tried and tested over many years, though they may not work for everyone, given different teaching styles, logistics, and available resources. At the least, you can modify from our framework according to your needs.

Class Preparation

Far too often we expect students to perform a task for which they are not adequately prepared. Forestry field studies will be entirely new to most students, so it is essential before conducting any exercise to have everyone on the same page. We cannot overemphasize how important preparation is to pulling off a successful field study. Discussions, readings, and videos should focus on giving students a basic understanding of the following (see Chapters 1 and 2):

- History of forestry, both local and national
- Principles of ecology, especially disturbances, secondary succession, and differentiation between tolerant (shade loving) and intolerant (sun-loving) species
- Values of the forests, including timber products, wildlife habitat, recreation, watershed protection, and biodiversity
- Principles of forestry and silviculture—the sustainable culture and managed growth of forests

Next, students need to be familiar with and know how to use the specialized equipment and instrumentation needed to collect data in the field. Students cannot be expected to conduct these studies successfully if they are using equipment for the first time. At minimum, the proper use of equipment must be demonstrated. Ideally, and if time permits, students should actually practice with the equipment prior to the first trip to the woods. For example, using a logger's tree scale stick is an important component of a woodlot study. This simple instrument determines the standing board feet in a tree. To practice prior to the trip, have the entire class do a reading on the school's flagpole as if it were a tree (Figures 3.1 and 3.2). Other instruments can be tested or calibrated on the school grounds and by using the trees growing there.

Finally, in preparation for the trip, the instructor should provide students with the parameters for the final report (see Chapter 8) based on their work in the field and the data they will collect. In fact, this should be the very first thing that is discussed about the actual field experience. Students should know exactly what is expected of them and the importance of communicating the results prior to conducting the work.

Selecting a Woodlot

Most schools are close to some sort of woodlot, either public or private, making a field study in forestry very feasible. In some states or counties, school districts actually own a tract of forest land. You don't need a large forested tract; a relatively small woodlot several acres in size will do as long as it is in a relatively natural state. A park, conservancy, or other natural area works perfectly (Figure 3.3). Make sure to get written approval from the appropriate authority or at least let them know what you are doing. A suitable woodlot on private land also is fine, provided the landowner gives written approval to use it. Whatever the size of the woods being used, the trees should be mature so their commercial aspects can be assessed and issues of forestry addressed. By *mature*, we mean that a significant number of trees should have diameters at breast height (DBH)[1] greater than 10 inches. Trees greater than 10 inches DBH are classified as saw timber, meaning they could be used for dimension lumber (such as 2 × 4s, 2 × 6s, 4 × 4s), plywood, or veneer.

Because a group size of five or six students will optimally engage all students in the field, select a forested area where you can define an adequate number of study plots for the number of groups you have. A perfect situation would be a forested area that contains stands of both coniferous and deciduous trees. Alternatively, a wooded area that consists of several different kinds of stands—older verus younger, upland verus lowland, ridge top verus valley bottom, or plantation versus natural—would provide a diversity that enriches the experience considerably for students

Figure 3.1. Student practicing with a tree scale stick by determining the height of the school's flagpole.

Figure 3.2. Student practicing with a tree scale stick by determining the "DBH" (diameter) of the school's flagpole.

Figure 3.3. Even a relatively small wooded area is a sufficient setting for these exercises.

Unless otherwise indicated, all photos by D. Glenn.

---

[1]Appendix B-2 gives various units of measurement used in forestry and their English-metric conversions

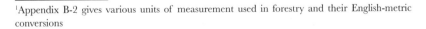

because of the comparisons that can be made. Future chapters will show how to record data from the different stands available. Of course, you will have to adapt your field studies to the natural resources in your locality and according to logistical limitations, particularly the availability of transportation.

The size of the woodlot is not terribly critical. As often is the case in data collection, bigger often is better because there will be a wider array of options in the location of study plots. The size of the woodlot has to be balanced with the time allotted, the size and number of the student work groups, and the forestry equipment and instruments available. For example, with a class of 30 students, divided into five groups of six students, working in two different stands (deciduous and coniferous) over a four-hour time frame, study plot areas of one-twentieth to one-fifth of an acre work fine[2]. In general, the larger the trees, the larger the study plots should be. But the exact size of study plots is not important and can be adjusted to meet both individual needs and the characteristics of the forest area being studied. However, the size of the plots must be known to convert data later to a per-acre basis, and all plots should be the same size.

Table 3.1. Suggested Plot Sizes for Forestry Field Studies

Fractional Acre	Area (sq. feet)	Dimensions (feet)	
		Square	Rectangular[*]
1/20	2,178	46.7 × 46.7	35 × 62.2
1/10	4,356	66 × 66	50 × 87.1
1/5	8,712	93.3 × 93.3	70 × 124.5

[*] Suggested dimensions. A rectangular plot could be any convenient dimensions that produce the required area.

A day or two prior to the study, the instructor should go to

[2]Units throughout this manual are given in English units, which is the standard for forestry and the wood products industry in the United States. For English-metric conversions, see Appendix B-2.

the woodlot and mark off the study plots. Each plot should be identified with a letter or number (Figure 3.4). Site lines on the perimeter of the plot can be marked using biodegradable flagging[3] (Figure 3.5). When laying out these plots you do not have to be precise to the nearest inch. Use two colors of flagging on the corners and one color to mark the perimeter. The number of study plots you mark will depend on how many student groups you have and if they can do two different kinds of forest stands (e.g., coniferous and deciduous) somewhat proximal to each other. For example, with a class of 30 students, with five groups of six students in an area with two different stands, mark six plots. During the study, place three of the five work groups in the deciduous, and two of the five in the coniferous stand. Then switch the groups at the appropriate time. If only one kind of forest stand is available, mark enough study plots so that each group can measure two widely separated plots to get an idea of the variation that exists across the area. Having lunch between the two plots is a great idea; it gives students a break, allows the instructor to check up on initial progress and correct any problems, and gives students a chance to regroup and get ready for their next study plot.

Figure 3.4. Study plot marker in a woodlot.

Figure 3.5. Biodegradable plastic flagging marks the perimeter of study plots.

Group Dynamics

Our experience with forestry field studies has shown that groups of six students are optimum. Determining the number of students per group will depend partially on how much time you have to spend in the field. With a smaller group—four students—more time in the field will be needed to collect all of the data. Other variables to consider are the size of the woodlot, the number of trees to be measured in each study plot, and the terrain. The key is to keep each student busy without giving them a workload that cannot be accomplished.

The instructor should determine the composition of the groups. Hopefully, you will know the personalities and abilities of the students by the time you do this exercise. Because many

---

[3]All equipment mentioned in this manual can be obtained from forestry or natural resource supply companies, such as Forestry Suppliers (*www.forestry-suppliers.com*) or Ben Meadows (*www.benmeadows.com*).

science classrooms have seating arrangements that pair a student with a partner, begin by selecting the strongest pairs. They become the core of each of the groups. Then match personalities and abilities as best you can to ensure each group will be productive in the field and the classroom.

At some point prior to the field trip, get the groups together so that they can begin to plan their work. One of the first things to be done is to have each group select a leader. This person then becomes a liaison between the instructor and the rest of the group. It is far easier to communicate with five group leaders in the field than 30 individual students. Group leaders also are given responsibility for keeping track of equipment and making sure that all work is completed and data recorded. Allow the group to choose their leader by whatever means they feel appropriate; you seldom will be disappointed in their choice.

One of the keys to a successful field study is the ability of team members to get along, know their assigned tasks, and work efficiently. Creation of a duties roster, whereby each student in the team commits to doing certain measurements or tasks is invaluable in optimizing time in the field. A roster avoids the problem of students standing around, hands in pockets, waiting for someone to do something; it immediately engages them in specific functions. However, students should be told that they need to be flexible, work as a team, and help others with their duties when they are finished with their own tasks. The roster, therefore, is not meant to be cast in cement but to be a functional guideline. An example of a duties roster involving a two-woodlot study (deciduous and coniferous) is given at the end of this chapter. The identifying letters or numbers of the plots that each group will work in should be given ahead of time, and these identifiers should be written on each group's duty roster.

Managing Equipment in the Field

As discussed earlier, your first objective regarding equipment and instrumentation is to familiarize students with equipment operation and the correct way to collect data in a field setting. The second objective—if your will budget allows—should be to make each group independent in terms of equipment. Each group should have all the equipment on-site that they need to measure their plots. Sharing equipment takes valuable time, is hard on the equipment, and can lead to conflicts. Shared equipment also is more likely to end up lost or unaccounted for.

The logistical problems associated with organizing equipment and moving it from classroom to bus, bus to field, and woodlot to woodlot should not be underestimated. Large plastic tubs, which are relatively inexpensive and readily available, work very well to minimize these problems (Figure 3.6). They also can function as a centralized station in the plots around which work is organized. Tubs also minimize misplacing equipment or leaving it behind or in a student's pocket or backpack.

Plastic tubs should be identified by number and each field study group should be assigned a number corresponding to a tub. Among other things, this system assures that there is some degree of accountability for equipment. Each tub should contain a list of the equipment and instruments it contains (see Appendix C). Laminating this list with plastic allows students to use water soluble markers to check off equipment at the end of the study and make notes about damaged equipment or other problems.

This is the digital age. If students have access to a digital camera or phone camera (but no incoming or outgoing calls allowed!), encourage them to bring it along to record their group's work or some interesting aspects of their study plots. The photo files are easily shared and they can add visual interest to the final report.

Figure 3.6. A readily available and inexpensive plastic tub contains the required equipment for a team doing a forestry field study.

Working in the Outdoors

For many students their first time working outdoors will be during this trip to the woods. Our experience is that some of them will not be prepared for the weather and conditions they will encounter. If it is cool, some will be underdressed; others will be wearing unsuitable shoes. If it should rain, raingear will be in short supply. The day before the field trip, make sure that each student goes home with a checklist of what to wear, including

- warm clothes (you can take a jacket off but can not put one on that you do not have);
- gloves if the weather will be cool;

Figure 3.7. Students should know how to identify and avoid poison ivy (shown here) and other plants that cause dermatitis.
Photo by D. Dickmann

- rugged footwear, preferably hiking boots or sturdy sneakers (absolutely no sandals or flip-flops, which almost guarantee foot injuries);
- long pants (no shorts); and
- rain gear unless there's no rain in the forecast.

The instructor must have a contingency plan in the event of bad weather on the day of the field trip. If possible, an alternate day should be scheduled as part of the plan. There is no sense in taking students out on a cold, snowy, or rainy day. The work will not get done or will be rushed; everyone will be miserable; and tempers will flare. Better to move ahead to a different classroom unit in the course and reschedule the field trip.

Insect repellant should be included in the equipment tubs, but students can bring their own, too. Forests are beautiful places, but mosquitoes, black flies, deer flies, ticks, and chiggers live there and can make life miserable. Some of these creatures also transmit diseases. Scheduling the trip in early spring before leaf-out or in the fall usually minimizes insect problems. In many places, plants that cause severe dermatitis—poison ivy, poison sumac, and poison oak—are common (Figure 3.7). Avoid areas where these plants grow in high concentrations, or at the least, warn students of their presence and make sure they know how to identify them.

Back in the Classroom and the Final Student Report

If possible, you should provide your students with several class periods following the field trip to analyze their data, develop sketches, and share data within their work groups (see Chapter 8). Students always should know prior to and during the field study exactly what will be expected of them in the final report. Initially, they might not understand all that is being asked of them, but once they are in the field, it all begins to make sense and have significance.

Forestry Study Duties Roster*

Group: #_____ Group Leader: _____

Recorders: _____ & _____

Study Plot # 1—Names	Task	Study Plot #2—Names
	Measure plot perimeter	
	Overhead sketch	
	Vertical structure sketch	
&	Age (DBH) class analysis	&
	Air & soil temperatures	
	Relative humidity	
&	Canopy cover	&
	Light intensity	
	Wind speed	
&	Ground cover density	&
&	Sawtimber board feet	&
&	Stocking D value	&
&	Stocking S value	&
Everyone	Observe wildlife habitat	Everyone
Everyone	Observe recreation	Everyone

*An ampersand (&) indicates that two people are required for the task. See Chapters 4 through 7 for descriptions of tasks.

CHAPTER 4
Vegetation Analysis

Mapping the structure of the vegetation in study plots is important for several reasons. First, with all the detailed data collected, students easily can lose perspective of the bigger picture; they can get lost in the trees and not see the forest, so to speak. By doing this analysis they will develop a three-dimensional perspective of their plots. Second, vegetative mapping provides students with a resource to better understand the data collected. The maps they produce might provide clues as to why aspects of the data collected may vary from point to point. Lastly, vegetative mapping provides the teacher with a road map of the plot against which other data, such as standing board feet or environmental information, can be cross-checked to validate student fieldwork.

Figure 4.1. Using a distance measuring wheel to determine the perimeter dimensions of a study plot.

Unless otherwise indicated, all photos by D. Glenn

Creating an Overhead Look

Students should create a sketch of their study plot as if they were looking at it from above, straight down. Using a distance measuring wheel (with brush guard) or a measuring tape, they should first record the length of each edge of the plot (Figure 4.1). Since the perimeter of the plot has already been flagged, they should easily be able to walk around the edges. Next, they should mark the locations and relative sizes of trees and shrubs on paper (Figure 4.2). Graph or engineering paper works best because a scale easily can be established on the paper, which helps in recording. Students should estimate the spread of each tree's leafy crown, as seen from below, and then sketch it in its proper location on the paper. Note the paradox of creating an overhead view by looking up from below (Figure 4.3). Be sure to emphasize that tree crowns frequently overlap and shrubs or small trees often underlie the crowns of large trees. Trees on a plot boundary are mapped if at least half of their trunk diameter is inside the plot, even if much of their crown lies outside the plot. It is very important that students survey their plot in a systematic way—for example, by zigzagging through it at set intervals—so that they do not miss any trees or map trees more than once.

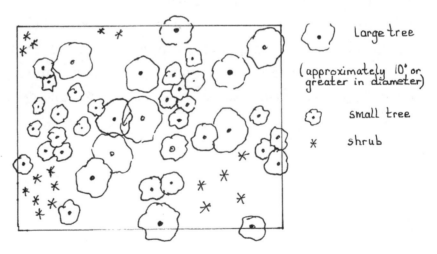

Figure 4.2. Hypothetical overhead map of a study plot showing the location of trees and shrubs of various sizes.

Defining Vertical Structure

Most woodlots consist of several vertical layers or **strata** of trees and shrubs. From the ground to the uppermost treetops, a typical profile would include (1) a low **understory**, (2) a **subcanopy** stratum of small suppressed or tolerant tree species, and (3) an **overstory** stratum. One of the first jobs a forester does in the analysis of a woodlot is to define the overstory stratum, which is occupied by the largest and most valuable trees (Figure 4.4). Trees that form the overstory stratum are referred to as **dominants** and **codominants**. Although there often is more than one canopy level in a stand, stands of pioneer species that come in after a severe disturbance or plantations simply may have an overstory and understory, with little in between (Figures 1.8, 1.11, and 1.13). The understory is made up of young tree seedlings and saplings (advance reproduction), small tree species, and shrubs (Figure 1.7). Sometimes a superdominant stratum above the general level of the overstory occurs (Figure 4.5; see also Figure 1.14).

Trees should not be included in a superdominant stratum unless they are considerably larger and clearly of an earlier generation than the trees of the main overstory. Occasionally a tree may be on the borderline between the overstory and subcanopy. If the tree offers significant competition to trees in the overstory (i.e., if its leaves or needles are touching or interlaced with those of the overstory trees), consider it part of the overstory.

Figure 4.3. The horizontal dimensions of a tree's crown usually can be estimated with reasonable accuracy from the ground, although it gets tricky when adjacent tree crowns overlap.
Photo by D. Dickmann.

Figure 4.4. Diagram of a hypothetical stratified forest stand. In young stands the subcanopy stratum may be missing.

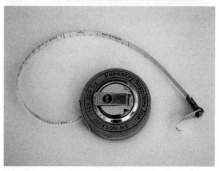

Figure 4.6. Instruments for measuring tree DBH. Top—tree calipers; bottom—diameter tape (D-tape).

Bottom photo by D. Dickmann.

To define the vertical stand structure of their study plots, students should make a drawing of the trees as if they were looking at the forest from one side (e.g., see Figures 1.10 and 1.16). This may be difficult to do because the profile of large trees is difficult to assess from ground level and the tops of the trees may not be visible. But students should do the best they can. Their drawings should resemble those in Figures 4.4 and 4.5 and be labeled in the same way. It is important that the crown for each visible tree be reflected in the sketch. Note that some crowns may be touching or even overlapping. Dead trees may be drawn if present, but they should be labeled as dead. All canopy strata—overstory, subcanopy, superdominants, understory—also should be labeled on the drawing.

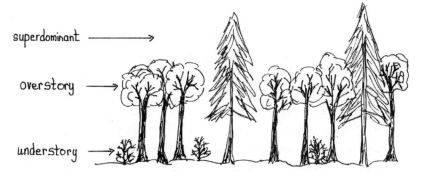

Figure 4-5. Diagram of a hypothetical stratified stand in which the upper stratum consists of large, widely spaced superdominant trees.

Tree Size Classification

The overhead and vertical structure of each study plot can be quantified to some degree by determining the size (DBH) class of each tree. These generalized size classes are related to some degree to tree age, although trees of the same diameter are rarely the same age. Students should use a caliper or diameter tape (Figures 4.6 and 4.7) to tally all the trees in each of their study plots according to their age class:

- Sapling (1 to 4 inches DBH)
- Poletimber (5 to 9 inches DBH)
- Sawtimber (10 inches or greater DBH)

This general classification has been useful in many ecology and forestry studies.

As an optional demonstration for each group, the instructor could use an increment borer to extract a core from a tree and have students count the growth rings to determine the age of the tree. The width of the rings also represents the year by year diameter growth rate of the tree. Increment borers are expensive, tricky to use, and easily damaged, so we do not recommend that students use them. Nonetheless, the demonstration could show students that tree ages and diameter growth rate are quantifiable without felling the tree, although the process is time-consuming and sometimes difficult.

Figure 4.7. Using tree calipers to determine tree DBH.

Study Plot Data Sheet—Age Class Classification

Age Class	Study Plot #1 Species or Forest Type		Study Plot #2 Species or Forest Type	
	# of Trees	Percentage of Total	# of Trees	Percentage of Total
Saplings (1–4 inches DBH)				
Poletimber (5–9 inches DBH)				
Sawtimber (10+ inches DBH)				
Total # of trees				

CHAPTER 5
The Abiotic and Biotic Forest Environment

The exercises in this chapter have a twofold purpose. First, they will characterize the abiotic environment (i.e., the microclimate created by the forest). It is important to realize that forests not only grow in response to the local climatic factors, but also create their own microclimate. Second, while trees are the dominant—and most eye-catching—life form in a forest ecosystem, many other organisms thrive in the microenvironment created by the trees. Two of the following exercises characterize the other plants that inhabit students' forest plots.

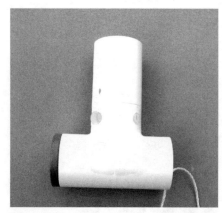

Figure 5.1. Densitometer used to determine overstory canopy cover.

Estimating Tree Canopy Cover

One of the most important indicators of the condition of a forest ecosystem and the microclimate it creates is crown closure or overstory tree canopy cover. Students will use an instrument called a densitometer[1] (Figure 5.1) to measure the tree canopy and—indirectly—the shade it produces. Data points will be taken along an imaginary triangle within the rectangular study plots (Figure 5.2). As students walk along this imaginary triangle they will take 100 sightings with the densitometer, approximately one-third along each side. A sighting with the densitometer is taken by looking into the base tube, making sure the vertical and horizontal levelers have the vial bubble centered, and reading the presence or absence of canopy via the mirror (Figure 5.3). Data will be recorded as either a "yes" (canopy foliage is seen) or "no" (sky is seen).

Because the data being collected using this technique is binomially distributed (i.e., for each sighting there is a "yes" or "no" answer; they see either mostly canopy overhead or mostly sky), a 100-sample point collection will convert directly to percent canopy coverage (as well as percentage sky coverage). For example, if 87 sightings are "yes", then the forest in the plot has 87% canopy cover.

---

[1]Equipment mentioned in this chapter is available from forestry or natural resource supply companies such as Forestry Suppliers (*www.forestry-suppliers.com*) or Ben Meadows (*www.benmeadows.com*).

Study Plot Data Sheet—Canopy Cover Tally

Study Plot #1 Species or Forest Type		Study Plot #2 Species or Forest Type	
Yes (canopy)	No (sky)	Yes (canopy)	No (sky)
Total count (% canopy cover)	Total count (% sky cover)	Total count (% canopy cover)	Total count (% sky cover)

Measuring the Abiotic Environment

Several measurements will be taken to characterize the abiotic environment of the study plots. All measurements will be taken at three designated locations or sample points within each plot (Figure 5.2), usually designated with plastic flagging (Figure 3.4). These sample points should be distributed so that they encompass the range of tree size-density, understory growth, and canopy cover that exists in the plot to account for as much of the spatial environmental variation in the plot as possible. Three points may well be insufficient to fully account for this variation—especially when measuring light intensity—but the constraints of time do not allow for more intensive sampling. Also, students will characterize the environment across a small time window during one day, so they cannot account for the day-to-day variation that occurs in the abiotic environment. Be sure that students are aware of this conundrum. Finally, a deciduous forest in full leaf will have a much different microclimate than one in the leafless condition; when the environmental data are analyzed and written up, the leaf condition of a deciduous forest needs to be noted up front.

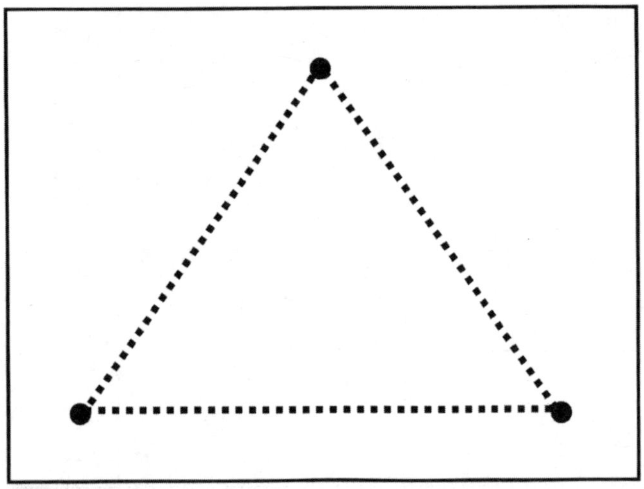

Figure 5.2. Location of three sampling points for measuring abiotic variables and route (dotted line) taken to determine canopy cover within a study plot.

Figure 5.3. Students taking data with a densitometer along a sampling route (see Figure 5.2) in their study plot.

Air and Soil Temperature

Recording air and soil temperatures provides students with a perfect example of how microhabitats provide different conditions for organisms at the same location. The difference between the air and soil temperatures can be quite striking. We really like digital thermometers with a probe (Figure 5.4). They are relatively inexpensive and work great for both air and soil temperatures. Additionally, they can be used in aquatic studies. But get ready for an inevitable question from students: "How long do I take the temperature?" The answer, of course, is until the temperature reading stabilizes or stays relatively constant. As with the other abiotic measurements, collect temperature data at the three designated sites within the study plots.

Figure 5.4. Recording soil temperature with a digital thermometer; note the probe inserted in the soil.

Study Plot Data Sheet—Air and Soil Temperature

	Study Plot #1 Species or Forest Type		Study Plot #2 Species or Forest Type	
	Air Temp. (°F or °C)	Soil Temp. (°F or °C)	Air Temp. (°F or °C)	Soil Temp. (°F or °C)
Time period during the day:				
Point A				
Point B				
Point C				
Average				
Range				

Relative Humidity

Relative humidity is an important environmental variable that represents the amount of water vapor in the air compared to the amount the air could hold at a certain temperature and barometric pressure—it represents the degree to which the air is saturated with water vapor. Relative humidity varies greatly from day to day, as well as over the course of a day, typically reaching a minimum in early afternoon and a maximum just before day break.

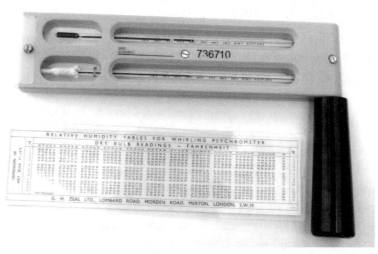

Figure 5.5. A sling psychrometer used to determine relative humidity.

To determine relative humidity a simple physical phenomenon is employed. When a fluid evaporates, it cools—when you get out of a hot shower, the water covering you starts to evaporate and immediately you feel a cooling effect. The less saturated the air is with water vapor (i.e., the lower the relative humidity), the faster the rate of evaporation and the greater the cooling effect. A hygrometer is the instrument used to determine relative humidity. The simplest hygrometer is the sling psychro-meter (Figure 5.5). Two thermometers are employed, one with no moisture on the bulb (the dry bulb) and one with a cloth wick soaked with distilled water (the wet bulb). In unsaturated air, evaporation from the cloth cools the wet bulb, giving a temperature lower than actual air temperature measured with the dry bulb thermometer. The greater the difference in temperature between the two thermometers, the lower the relative humidity. By consulting a table of wet and dry bulb temperatures (supplied with the psychrometer), the data can be converted easily to relative humidity.

Students use the sling psychrometer to determine relative humidity at the three designated locations (sample points) within each study plot. Make sure they whirl the psychrometer long enough (usually a minute or two) for constant wet and dry bulb temperatures to be reached (Figure 5.6). Relative humidity (in percent) is recorded at each point and then the average for the plot is computed.

Figure 5.6. Student whirling a sling psychrometer in a study plot.

Study Plot Data Sheet—Relative Humidity, Light Intensity, and Wind Velocity

Environmental Variables	Study Plot #1 Species or Forest Type		Study Plot #2 Species or Forest Type	
Relative humidity (%)—Time period during the day:				
Point A				
Point B				
Point C				
Average				
Range				
Light intensity (e.g., Lux)—Time period during the day:				
Point A				
Point B				
Point C				
Average				
Range				
Wind velocity (mph)—Time period during the day:				
	3 ft (1 m) height	6 ft (2 m) height	3 ft (1 m) height	6 ft (2 m) height
Point A				
Point B				
Point C				
Average				
Range				

Light Intensity

Few abiotic factors surpass light intensity in importance, because light drives the life-giving process of photosynthesis. At low-light levels, photosynthesis proceeds slowly, perhaps not fast enough to keep some plants alive and allowing little or no energy and carbon to be stored in an ecosystem. The reverse is true under high-light levels, and most plants thrive under these conditions. However, within the great diversity of the plant kingdom are

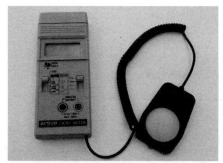

Figure 5.7. A digital meter to measure light intensity in lux.

species that have become adapted to low-light levels, and these plants typically can be found growing in the shade at ground level (i.e., in the understory) beneath a forest stand.

Even within small communities, light intensity can vary considerably from place to place because the overstory tree canopy and subcanopy are porous. Furthermore, a given spot on the forest floor receives different amounts of light during the day as the Sun moves across the sky. Another source of variability is intermittent cloud cover, where one minute a spot may be in bright sunlight and in low-intensity diffuse light the next. On a day with uniform cloud cover, not only is overall light intensity lower, but variation in intensity is smaller from place to place and time to time. Thus, the light intensity regime of a forest is difficult to characterize because of extreme spatial and temporal variations. The practical bottom line is this: Take light measurements over as many sample points, over as many times of a given day, and on as many days as possible.

To measure light intensity, a light meter[2] (Figure 5.7) is held at about waist level with the sensing window pointing exactly upward. Students should be sure that their shadow does not interfere with the reading. Light intensity is recorded at the three sample points in each study plot[3] (Figure 5.8). These points should take in as much variation in light conditions as possible. If a deciduous woodlot is surveyed when the trees are in the leafless condition, the meter readings should be taken in the shadow of a few large trees as well as in areas where there is no shade.

Students should be able to notice changes in understory vegetation corresponding to available light. Plants that are exposed to low light intensities show adaptations to that environment. For example, they may have broad leaves to trap the little light that reaches them. Vegetation in heavily shaded areas may be scant and scattered. Students should watch for such variations as they perform this study.

Figure 5.8. Student using a digital meter to take a light intensity reading. The ribbon denotes one of three sample points where abiotic data are collected within a study plot.

[2]Many kinds of light meters are available from environmental, forestry, and natural resource supply companies. These meters quantify light using several different units (foot-candles, lumens, lux, watts per m[2], etc.). Although the exact kind of meter or the units it records does not particularly matter for this exercise, we recommend a digital meter that measures in lux.

[3]The extreme temporal and spatial variability in light intensity under a forest canopy would require many more sample points—as well as several sets of measurements across the course of a day—to fully characterize the light environment. But the limitations of time usually will preclude a more intensive sampling.

Wind Velocity

Forests are windbreaks. On a windy day you might have to hold onto your hat in the open, but walk inside a dense forest stand and it will be relatively calm. These data will characterize wind velocity within the study plots. To be accurate, the anemometer (Figure 5.9) should be held for 10 seconds and then wind velocity (mph) recorded. To test if a stratification of wind velocity exists, measure it at heights of 3 feet (1 m) and 6 feet (2 m). The above procedure is repeated at each of the three sample points in each plot. Make sure students do not block the wind when taking measurements!

Figure 5.9. An anemometer for measuring wind velocity.

Optional Exercises

If only one kind of forest is available for study, the following exercises can be done to round out the day of fieldwork. They illustrate some very important ecological principles. An even better alternative is to have the students suggest additional exercises during the classroom preparatory session.

> The pronounced effect that a forest canopy in full leaf has on understory microclimate can be demonstrated if the same abiotic measurements discussed above also are taken in an open area. If a field, prairie, or meadow exists close to the forest study plots (even a parking lot will do, though soil temperatures cannot be taken), and if time is available, students can do a complete set of abiotic measurements there. The comparisons will be striking!

> Another optional exercise is to characterize the **ecotone**—the boundary zone between a forest and an open area (Figure 5.10). Within this zone, which can extend into the forest and open area for many feet, the forest modifies the open environment, which in turn modifies the forest environment. This is the zone of edge effect. An ecotone usually contains a higher diversity of plants and animals than either of the adjacent communities because there are more habitats or ecological niches. Students take abiotic measurements at the forest-open area edge and then 20 to 50

Figure 5.10. The ecotone between a mature hardwood forest and an open field.

Photo by D. Dickmann.

feet (or about half the height of the tallest trees) into the forest and into the field to characterize the ecotone. The data is then be compared to data from the forest interior.

Estimating Understory Plant Density

The understory microclimate creates a habitat for the many organisms besides overstory trees that inhabit a forest ecosystem, from the lowliest bacterium to complex plants and animals. In this exercise students will measure the density of forest floor plants that are adapted to the microenvironment of the study plots. These plants will be sampled by setting down a line of 10 subplots across each study plot (Figure 5.11). These subplots should be 3.3 feet on a side (10.9 feet^2 or 1/4000th of an acre and exactly equivalent to 1 m^2). All plants with stems ½-inch (1 cm) thick or less are counted within each subplot. Square frames of plastic pipe (10.9 feet^2) are dropped on the ground along the sampling line to designate the boundary of each subplot (Figure 5.12). These frames can be assembled and disassembled easily to fit into the plastic equipment tubs. Data will be expressed as the average of the 10 samples (plants per subplot).

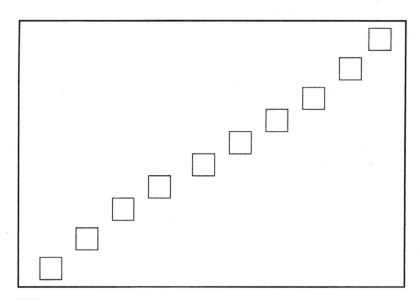

Figure 5.11. Sampling pattern for assessing understory plant density in a study plot. Each square represents a 3 × 3 foot (10.6 feet^2 or 1/4000 acre or 1 m^2) sample subplot; subplots are spaced about 12 feet apart.

☐ One sampling subplot

While not required, if students have knowledge of plant identification, they can take notes on the different species present in each subplot. A more quantitative approach would be to determine species richness. Begin by counting the number of different species in the first plot, identifying them as species #1, species #2 and so on. If the real name of a species is known, it could be recorded (e.g., sword fern, trillium, or blueberry). The presence of *additional* species would be recorded in the nine successive plots. Summing the total number of species recorded over the 10 plots would give species richness, a measure of diversity. Additional measures of diversity are used by ecologists—the Shannon Index and the Simpson Index—but their calculation is complicated and requires taking much more detailed data than is practical in this exercise.

An option to measuring the density of understory plants is to estimate ground cover, the percentage of the area of each subplot (when viewed from above) occupied by plant foliage. Because it is just an ocular estimate, just use percentages to the tens place (i.e., 10%, 20%, 30%, and so on). This method is preferable when grasses, multiple-stemmed plants, or trailing plants occupy much of the understory, because estimating the number of stems can be nearly impossible. On the other hand, density is preferred when understory plants are mostly single-stemmed or in the leafless condition, or when plants with many stems are infrequent.

Figure 5.12. Determining understory plant density. The 3.3- × 3.3-foot (1 m²) subplot frame is made from ¾-inch PVC plastic conduit that can be easily assembled and disassembled on-site.

Study Plot Data Sheet—Understory Plant Ground Cover Density (or Ground Cover)

Subplots	Study Plot #1 Species or Forest Type	Study Plot #2 Species or Forest Type
	# of plants per subplot (1/4000th acre)*	
A		
B		
C		
D		
E		
F		
G		
H		
I		
J		
Average		
Range		
Plants species noted (optional)		

* Or percentage cover if density is difficult to determine.

CHAPTER 6
Measuring Commercial Timber Values

This chapter outlines certain procedures used by foresters to measure the amount or volume of timber (primarily sawlogs) in a forest stand. This process is called **timber inventory**. Just as a storeowner keeps track of the inventory of stock on hand at a particular time, so does a forest landowner keep track of his or her timber stock. Additionally, the landowner may use the data from an inventory to prescribe certain silvicultural treatments that can promote optimal timber growth.

Determination of Stand Density

A crucial piece of data for the effective management of forests is **stand density**—an estimate of how many trees are growing on a given unit of land area. Stand density usually is expressed as number of trees per acre (or per hectare). Tables have been developed by foresters to show density levels for optimum timber production for a particular combination of tree species (or type of forest) and soil. In this exercise students can compare the actual measured density with the optimum density, then include in their management plan the means by which this ideal density can be achieved (e.g., by thinning out some of the trees).

The basic formula employed is:

$$\textbf{D} + \textbf{X} = \textbf{S}$$

where **D** is the average DBH of trees in the stand, **X** is a stocking variable (that varies with tree species or forest type), and **S** is the average spacing or distance between trees.

The following data are required to determine stand density (use the study plot data sheet for stand density as a guide):

> Measure the distance between trees in the study plots using a tape measure (Figure 6.1). Include all trees 5 inches DBH or greater. An average spacing distance is determined for each plot—the **S** value in the equation.

> Measure the DBH of trees in each study plot ≥5 inches DBH using a tree caliper (Figures 4.6 and 4.7), diameter tape, or tree scale stick[1]. An average diameter is found for each plot—the **D** value in the equation.

Having the **S** value (average spacing or distance between trees), you can use Table 6.1 (Average Tree Spacing and Equivalent Density, p. 59) to determine the current stand density. For example, if the average distance between trees in a study plot comprising principally oak trees is 16 feet (S = 16), Table 6.1 shows that a spacing of 16 feet equates to 170 trees per acre.

Figure 6.1. Measuring the distance between trees. These data are then used to obtain the "**S**" value in the stand density exercise.

Unless otherwise indicated, all photos by D. Glenn.

[1]Equipment mentioned in this chapter is available from forestry or natural resource supply companies such as Forestry Suppliers (*www.forestry-suppliers.com*) or Ben Meadows (*www.benmeadows.com*).

To determine the ideal density for a stand, refer to Table 6.2 (Guide for Determing Optimum Tree Spacing, p. 59). If, for example, in that same oak study plot, the average tree DBH was 10 inches (D = 10), Table 6.2 indicates that at an average DBH of 10 inches, oaks should be stocked at D + 9. Substituting D = 10 and X = 9 in the equation, we arrive at a new S_1 value of 19 (10 + 9 = 19). Look back to Table 6.1 and find that at an S_1 of 19 feet, the optimum density should be 121 trees per acre.

The original S value—the current or existing density of trees in the plot—equated to 170 trees per acre. The new or optimum density (S_1) was calculated to be 121 trees per acre. Therefore, there are 49 trees per acre too many to maximize production of large-diameter, sawlog trees:

$$\begin{array}{r} 170 \text{ trees per acre is the existing density} \\ -\underline{121} \text{ trees per acre is the "optimum" density} \\ 49 \text{ trees per acre in excess} \end{array}$$

Therefore, the prescription in the management plan would be to remove 49 trees per acre in a thinning. Usually the smallest and poorest quality trees (crooked, forked, having broken tops or large branches, rotten) or tree species of low value would be the ones thinned out. However, trees that provide good wildlife habitat (e.g., den trees) or food (e.g., oaks with acorns, hickories with nuts, wild cherry with soft fruit) often will not be removed, even if they are of poor timber quality. Overall diversity of tree species also should not be appreciably reduced.

Significance of Stand Density

Imagine that you planted a row of carrot seeds one-quarter inch apart and nearly all of the seeds germinated. That may excite the novice gardener, but if your object is to harvest carrots similar to those you purchase at a grocery store, then those crowded carrots are going to be a disappointment. To get long, thick carrots, that row would have to be thinned out, maybe several times. In like fashion, foresters interested in increasing the production of high-quality sawtimber would need to thin out the forest to produce tall, straight, large-diameter trees.

CHAPTER 6
Measuring Commercial Timber Values

Figure 6.2. Forest stand in British Columbia thinned to optimum stand density.

There are many variables to consider when determining the appropriate density for a given stand—species or forest type, the age of the stand, the productivity potential of the soil, and the products the landowner wants from that stand (Figure 6.2). The study we propose simply but accurately provides the necessary information for students to develop prescriptions to optimize timber production by altering stand density.

Table 6.1. Average Tree Spacing (Left, In Feet) and Equivalent Density (Right, in Number of Trees Per Acre [TPA])

3' – 4,840 TPA	11' – 360 TPA	19' – 121 TPA	28' – 55 TPA
4' – 2,722 TPA	12' – 304 TPA	20' – 109 TPA	30' – 48 TPA
5' – 1,742 TPA	13' – 258 TPA	21' – 99 TPA	32' – 42 TPA
6' – 1,210 TPA	14' – 222 TPA	22' – 90 TPA	36' – 34 TPA
7' – 888 TPA	15' – 194 TPA	23' – 83 TPA	40' – 27 TPA
8' – 681 TPA	16' – 170 TPA	24' – 76 TPA	45' – 22 TPA
9' – 538 TPA	17' – 151 TPA	25' – 70 TPA	50' – 17 TPA
10' – 436 TPA	18' – 135 TPA	26' – 65 TPA	60' – 12 TPA

Table 6.2. Guide (D + X Values) for Determining Optimum Tree Spacing[a]

Average DBH (inches)	Oaks and Other Dry-Mesic[b] Hardwoods	Pines and Douglas Fir	Northern or Mesic[b] Hardwoods	Spruce, Fir, or Hemlock
6	D + 7	D + 6	D + 6	D + 4
8	D + 8	D + 6	D + 7	D + 4
10	D + 9	D + 6	D + 8	D + 4
12	D + 10	D + 6	D + 9	D + 4
14	D + 11	D + 6	D + 9	D + 4
16	D + 11	D + 6	D + 10	D + 4
18	D + 12	D + 8	D + 10	D + 6
20	D + 12	D + 8	D + 11	D + 6

[a]In stands of a mixture of conifers and hardwoods, use the D + X value that corresponds to the most prevalent species.

[b]*Dry mesic* refers to soils that are somewhat dry and moderately fertile; *mesic* refers to moist, fertile soils.

Study Plot Data Sheet: Stand Density

Stand Density Data	Study Plot #1 Species or Forest Type	Study Plot #2 Species or Forest Type
Current average S (feet)		
Current average D (inches)		
Current density (trees per acre)		
Stocking value (X)		
Optimum S_1 (= D + X)		
Optimum density (trees per acre)		
Number of trees to be thinned out (current density-optimum density)		

Determination of Standing Board Feet Using the Tree and Log Scale Stick

To develop a management plan for timber production, a forester must assess the commercial value of sawtimber. This can be done several ways, depending on available equipment. The simplest method with acceptable accuracy is use of the tree and log scale stick or the "forester's slide rule." This ingenious device can do a number of measurements and data conversions, yet it is compact, inexpensive, and easy to use. In this exercise two tree dimensions need to be determined with the stick: DBH and merchantable height. To measure DBH, hold the side of the stick labeled TREE SCALE STICK at arm's length (about 25 inches) horizontally against the tree at breast height. Close one eye and visually line up the zero (left) end of the scale with one side of the tree. At the point where the line of vision in the opposite direction intersects the other side of the tree, read the DBH (up to 40 inches) along the scale on top of the stick (Figures 6.3, 6.4, and 6.5). Be sure to measure only trees that are living.

To measure merchantable height, stand at a distance of 66 feet (1 chain) from the tree (use a tape measure or stretch a 66-foot

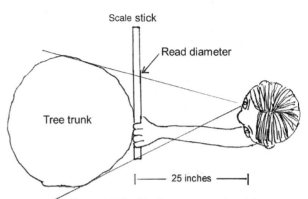

Figure 6.3. Positioning a tree scale stick against a tree trunk at breast height to determine its DBH.

Figure 6.4. Student using a tree scale stick to determine the diameter of a tree at breast height (DBH).

A. To determine the diameter (DBH) of a tree use the top scale.

TREE SCALE STICK INTERNATIONAL 1/4" RULE (FC-78) HOLD STICK LEVEL 25 INCHES FROM EYE AGAINST TREE AT HEIGHT OF 4-1/2 FEET, READ AVERAGE TREE VOLUME IN BOARD FEET	DIAMETER OF TREE (INCHES)	10	11	12	13	14
	1 16 FOOT LOG	36	46	56	67	78
	2 16 FOOT LOGS	59	76	92	112	132
	3 16 FOOT LOGS	73	96	120	147	174
	4 16 FOOT LOGS			137	168	200
	5 16 FOOT LOGS					

B. To determine the merchantable height of a tree use this edge.

STAND 66 FEET FROM TREE PLUMB STICK 25 INCHES FROM EYE LINE UP END OF STICK WITH STUMP HEIGHT, READ NUMBER 16 FOOT LOGS   1   MERRITT HYPSOMETER   2

C. To determine the number of board feet in a tree use the tree DBH and the matrix below the diameter scale (same side as A above).

TREE SCALE STICK INTERNATIONAL 1/4" RULE (FC-78) HOLD STICK LEVEL 25 INCHES FROM EYE AGAINST TREE AT HEIGHT OF 4-1/2 FEET, READ AVERAGE TREE VOLUME IN BOARD FEET	DIAMETER OF TREE (INCHES)	10	11	12	13	14
	1 16 FOOT LOG	36	46	56	67	78
	2 16 FOOT LOGS	59	76	92	112	132
	3 16 FOOT LOGS	73	96	120	147	174
	4 16 FOOT LOGS			137	168	200
	5 16 FOOT LOGS					

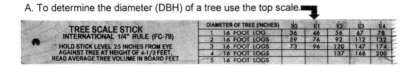

Figure 6.5. How to read the tree scale stick to determine tree DBH, merchantable height, and volume.

CHAPTER 6
Measuring Commercial Timber Values

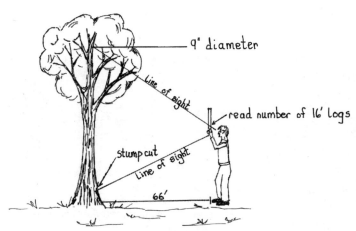

Figure 6.6. How to use the Merritt hypsometer scale on the tree scale stick to determine the merchantable height of a tree.

Figure 6.7. Student determining the merchantable height of a tree (in number of 16-foot logs) with the Merritt hypsometer scale of the tree scale stick.

precut string) (Figure 6.6). On sloping ground it is best to stay approximately on the same level or contour as the base of the tree. Hold the tree scale stick vertically, about 25 inches from the eye, with the narrow side labeled MERRITT HYPSOMETER facing the operator (Figures 6.6 and 6.7). Close one eye and visually line up the zero (bottom) end of the scale with the stump height (the point where the logger would most likely cut the tree, usually 1 to 2 feet above ground). Then, holding steady, sight to the top of the usable trunk length, usually at the point where the diameter of the tree is about 9 inches (8 inches inside the bark, the minimum small end size for a sawlog) or where a major fork or other defect limits merchantability.[2] At that point the logger would "top" the tree. Where the line of vision intersects with the stick scale and the merchantable top of the tree, a number is read (between one and six). Each number on this part of the scale represents 16-foot logs (e.g., a reading of "three" on this scale would mean three 16-foot logs). A little practice beforehand (Figures 3.1 and 3.2, p. 29) will enhance commercial tree height measurements in the field.

Now that students have two tree dimensions—DBH and number of logs—they can use the side of the stick labeled TREE SCALE STICK (the same side that was used to measure DBH) to cross matrix the DBH and the number of 16-foot logs to get the volume of the tree in board feet.[3] For example, using the stick shown in Figure 6.5, a tree with a DBH of 12 inches and a mer-

[2] Estimating merchantable top height is the most difficult part of this exercise; basically, the minimum 9-inch diameter must be estimated by eye, which takes some practice to do accurately. If merchantable height is limited by forks, large branches, or defects, this diameter estimation may not be necessary. However, sometimes a large branch or fork may occur low enough that a 16-foot log or two could be taken out above it. See the following link for more information on estimating tree volume and merchantable height: *www.midnr.com/Publications/pdfs/ForestsLandWater/TimberSaleReports/App.08ProductStandars7-30-2004.pdf*

[3] Tree and log scale sticks are available in three versions: Doyle, Scribner, and International ¼. These versions represent different formulas (called log rules) for computing the volume of a tree based on its DBH and the number of 16-foot logs it contains. Check with your local cooperative extension agent; consulting forester; forestry school; or industrial, state, or federal forestry office to learn which log rule is used in your area.

chantable height of two logs would have a volume of 92 board feet; a 14-inch, three-log tree would contain 174 board feet.

The clinometer is an alternate tool to the Merritt hypso-meter for determining tree height (Figure 6.8). You might want to have students try using a clinometer, although they are con-siderably more expensive than a tree scale stick. This optical in-strument also requires that the observer stand a certain distance from the tree (usually 66 or 100 feet, depending on the model). The merchantable height limit of the tree (or very top of the tree) is sighted through the eyepiece, and the height in feet is read directly. This measurement can then be converted to number of 16-foot logs. One of the advantages of using this tool is that it easily compensates for slope. For areas that are not level, this may be a significant advantage. The clinometer is much more versatile than the hypsometer because it can measure the height of any object or the angle of a slope or incline.

Sophisticated electronic equipment also is available from forestry supply companies to measure tree dimensions. Laser-based hypsometers, range finders, combination range finder/hypsometers, and calipers greatly increase the ease and accuracy of these measurements. Data are automatically recorded for later downloading to a computer. Although this equipment is too expen-sive for routine student use, if funds are available for a single purchase the instructor might use these tools for demonstration.

Figure 6.8. A clinometer is an alternative instrument for measuring merchantable tree height or the height of any object. Photo by D. Dickmann.

Defects

In forestry as well as in other commercial enterprises, all that glitters is not necessarily gold. A tree at first glance may appear healthy, but may in fact be under attack from insects and diseases (pests), most of which are natural and important members of any ecosystem. Additionally, introduced non-native pests from other parts of the world—white pine blister rust, emerald ash borer, hemlock wooly adelgid, to name just a few—have deva-stated forests in certain parts of North America. So when a for-ester conducts an inventory in a woods, he or she must look for signs of insect and disease attack and subtract the damage they have done—called *defect*—from the overall volume of the stand, a procedure that requires some experience. Dead trees are not

Figure 6.9. Many old trees are infested with heart rot fungi, which eat out the center of the tree. But if the outer growth rings are intact, the tree will live and appear healthy, although it will be more susceptible to wind breakage. Photo by D. Dickmann.

Figure 6.10. Meandering galleries made by larvae of the invasive emerald ash borer feeding on the innermost bark of an ash tree (the bark has been stripped off). In the process the larvae girdled the tree and killed it.

Photo by D. Dickmann.

Figure 6.11. This beech tree is infested with heart rot, indicated by the fungal sporophytes (conks) on the bark. The rotted portion of the lower trunk is unusable and would be subtracted as defect from the total volume of the tree.

Photo by D. Dickmann.

tallied at all. Defect could be pest-caused crooks, forks, other disfigurements, or stem decay, which causes heart rot (Figure 6.9). The warning signs of imminent death of trees from pests also are noted and may invoke a decision to harvest trees before they are killed (Figure 6.10).

Although students will not subtract defect from their tree volumes in this exercise, they should take note nonetheless of signs of insect and disease attack. Are trees malformed or disfigured because of damage to the growing points (e.g., due to attack by the white pine weevil)? Are cankers (areas of dead bark) or fungal sporophytes (conks) that indicate heart rot present on the trunk (Figure 6.11)? If the tree is a pine or other conifer, are there pitch blisters on the bark that indicate bark beetle infestation? Has the bark been scraped off due to some kind of machine damage?

Significance of Tree Volume

For a landowner to realize the economic value in a tract of forest, an estimate of the amount of wood that the forest has grown is necessary. This estimate can then be used as the basis of a timber sale or a timber harvest. A private landowner could then advertise this information to local loggers, who would submit bids for a timber sale. For a timber company owning forest land that supplies logs to one of their mills, this information would be used to plan for a continual supply of raw material to that mill. Another reason for inventory data would be a land sale; the value of the timber on that land would be a large factor in determining its selling price. Finally, the U.S. Forest Service and various natural resource agencies assemble inventory data on a state, regional, or national level for planning purposes.

After logs are sawn into lumber, that lumber typically is bought and sold at a certain price per board foot. A call or visit to a local lumberyard or home supply store will allow students to obtain the current retail price per board foot of the dominant species in their study plots. They can then compute the retail value of individual trees and begin to realize why trees are harvested and understand the economic basis for the timber industry.

Study Plot Data Sheet: Tree Volume

Study Plot #_____ Species (or Forest Type) _____

Tree #	DBH (Inches)	# of 16-Foot Logs	Volume (Board Feet)
1			
2			
3			
4			
5			
6			
7			
8			
9			
10			
11			
12			
Etc. as required			
		Total board feet	
Notes on defects			

CHAPTER 7
Recreation and Wildlife

In the foreword to *A Sand County Almanac*, Aldo Leopold observed, "There are some who can live without wild things, and some who cannot." Many of the people who need "wild things" are drawn to forests. An indication of the magnitude of this draw is found in data compiled by the U.S. Forest Service (*www. fs.fed.us/recreation/programs/nvum*): In fiscal year 2007, there were more than 178.6 million visits to national forests across the United States; 86% of them were for recreational purposes! Forests of all kinds provide humans with a wide range of wildland recreational opportunities, which greatly increases the value of forests in contemporary life (Figures 1.22 and 7.1). In fact, many private and public forests are managed primarily for recreation, including watching wildlife, hunting, and fishing (Figure 7.2).

Figure 7.1. For people with an inclination toward the natural world, the beauty and biological diversity of forested places offer an irresistible draw.
Photo by D. Glenn.

Figure 7.2. Forests always have provided sports people with great fishing and hunting.

Unless otherwise indicated, all photos by D. Dickmann.

CHAPTER 7
Recreation and Wildlife

Figure 7.3. A simple path, which is easy to construct and maintain, enhances the recreational value of a forest during all seasons of the year.

Recreational Use

While students are working in their study plots, they should observe and consider the following recreational aspects of the overall forest area.

Current Use: How is this area used? Are there hiking, ski, bicycle, and horseback trails (Figures 7.3 and 7.4); campsites; or a picnic area? Anything to indicate hunting of legal game? Any possibilities for fishing? Archeological or historic sites (Figures 1.1 and 7.5)? Does the area have a nature center, shelters, or signage (Figure 7.6)?

Unique Aspects: Are there any visually unique areas within the forest area (e.g., a waterfall, pond, or stream [Figure 1.22], picturesque lookout points, or places of solitude)?

Aesthetic Aspects: Comment on the overall aesthetics of the forest area. Is it a pleasant place? Do you feel drawn toward it or are you indifferent to it? Specifically, what do you like and dislike about it?

Figure 7.4. Trail riders of all kinds, be they on horseback, bicycles, or off-road motorized vehicles, find forested trails irresistible.

Photo courtesy of Hoof Prints Trail Riding Center, Wicomico Demonstration Forest/Chesapeake Forest, Parsonsburg, MD.

Figure 7.5. In many areas, historic or archeological structures—here a log cabin built by Finnish pioneers—provide points of interest and opportunities for study in a forest tract.

Figure 7.6. Well-designed and -located signage improves the learning experience of visitors to a recreational area.

Study Plot Data Sheet: Recreational Aspects

Recreational Aspects	Study Plot #1 Species or Forest Type		Study Plot #2 Species or Forest Type	
	Current	Future?	Current	Future?
Camping				
Picnicking				
Fishing				
Hunting				
Watching wildlife				
Hiking				
Bicycling				
Off-road vehicles				
Horseback riding				
Historic or archeological sites				
Nature center				
Interpretative signs				
Other				
Unique features				
Visual features				

Forests as Habitats for Wildlife

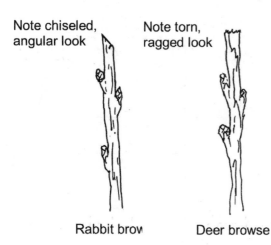

Note chiseled, angular look

Note torn, ragged look

Rabbit brow

Deer browse

Figure 7.7. Animals leave characteristic evidence of their feeding habits. The cleanly cut stem on the left was browsed by a rabbit with sharp upper and lower incisors. The stem on the right was browsed by a deer, which has no upper incisors but rather a leathery upper palate, causing a tearing action.

When considering the management of forestlands, one may find issues pertaining to wildlife habitat to be very significant to, if not the driving force behind management plans and recreational use. Consider, for example, the influence that endangered or threatened animal species have had on the management of forests. To protect the habitat for the endangered northern spotted owl, harvesting of old-growth timber in the Pacific Northwest has been halted. Throughout the South, management of longleaf pine forests is determined largely by the presence or absence of breeding colonies of the endangered red-cockaded woodpecker. Another wildlife issue that has generated much controversy is management of habitat for white-tailed deer in the eastern United States. Foresters and ecologists insist that there are too many deer in many areas and deer should be managed *against* to insure the long-term sustainability of the forest.

One of the problems students have when evaluating the current wildlife diversity of a woods is the misplaced thinking that "If I don't see it, it doesn't exist." Obviously, when your troop

Figure 7.8. Indirect evidence of wildlife activity can be just as convincing as direct sightings. Above left: Fecal droppings (scat) of white-tailed deer. Above right: A great horned owl regurgitated this pellet containing the fur and bones of a small rodent.

of students arrives at a forest site, most animals disappear quickly. Therefore, students need to look mostly for *indirect* evidence of wildlife (Figures 7.7 and 7.8)—tracks, burrows, nests, fecal droppings (scat), browsing damage, skeletal remains, or predatory evidence (e.g., owl pellets or partially consumed animal carcasses)—in addition to actual animal sightings (Figure 7.9).

You should emphasize that everyone in the team needs to look continually for evidence of wildlife. This sounds simple, but most of us who have worked with students continue to be amazed at what they don't see. As Aldo Leopold observed in *A Sand County Almanac*, "The deer hunter watches the next bend; the duck hunter watches the skyline; the bird hunter watches the dog; the non-hunter does not watch." In other words, what a person sees in the outdoors often is based on why they chose to be there in the first place. A corollary is that if you have observed something in one place (e.g., an owl pellet), you are much more likely to look for it in another. Just another way of saying that experience counts!

Figure 7.9. However fleeting, nothing beats a direct sighting of a wild animal, here a great egret.

Study Plot Data Sheet—Wildlife* Evidence

Study Plot #1   Species or Forest Type:

Animal Species	Evidence	Frequency (# of Sightings or Observations)

Study Plot #2   Species or Forest Type:

Animal Species	Evidence	Frequency (# of Sightings or Observations)

*Includes birds, amphibians, reptiles, mammals—anything that flies, walks, or crawls.

Exclosures

If a permanent site for these forest exercises is available, and if time, money, and ownership approval allow, a long-term study can be established to determine the impact of grazers and browsers on understory habitat. Exclosures are fenced plots to keep large herbivore animals out (Figure 7.10). The fencing in larger exclosures needs to be at least 8 to 10 feet high (e.g., two layers of stock fence) and sturdily built to withstand the rigors of the environment, animal damage, and even vandalism. A gate is required for access. Exclosures can range from several square feet to many acres in size. Control (unfenced) plots of similar size and composition should be established close to the exclosures for comparison. The long-term effects on understory plant communities of protection from browsing and grazing often are striking. After the exclosures have had their effect, students could collect data on the density of plant growth, the diversity of plant species, and the diameter and height of woody stems both inside and outside the exclosures.

Figure 7.10. A fenced-in exclosure designed to prevent large herbivores (e.g., deer, moose, elk) from browsing young trees. Note the height of the fence (about 10 feet).

CHAPTER 8
After the Field Study

Out of the Field, Back in the Classroom

If possible, provide your students with several class periods subsequent to the field trip to analyze data, make computations, develop sketches, and share data within work groups. Two hours is probably adequate. Part of this time should be spent cleaning the equipment boxes and using the equipment checklists to identify any deficiencies and needed repairs or replacements.

To help students focus on all the computations, sketches, charts, and data they need to construct and write the report, we like to provide them with a Forestry Data Summary Sheet. This simple document has proven exceptionally effective for helping students focus on the task and guiding them efficiently toward the end product—the final report.

Forestry Data Summary Sheet

Your report on the forest field study must contain all of the following drawings, data sets, and observations for each of your study plots. Most of these data should already be entered in the **Study Plot Data Sheets.**

1. Drawings <u>with key</u> (graph or engineering paper):
    *   Overhead stand view
    *   Vertical stand structure
2. Age class analysis—percentage sapling, pole timber, and sawtimber
3. Averaged abiotic data—do not forget the units!
    *   Air temperature (°F or °C)
    *   Soil temperature (°F or °C)
    *   Relative humidity (%)
    *   Wind speed (mph)
    *   Light intensity (Lux)
    *   Canopy cover (%)
    *   Ground cover density (stems per plot) or percentage ground cover
4. Stand density—do not forget the units!
    *   Give actual D and S values.
    *   Give current density using actual S
    *   Using $D + X = S$, determine the new S_1 value. Show your work!
    *   What is the optimum stand density (S_1)?
5. Sawtimber
    *   Show sawtimber data, giving DBH, merchantable height (# of 16-foot logs) and board feet per tree
    *   Compute total board feet for the plot.
6. Evidence of recreation: List observations for overall study area.
7. Evidence of wildlife: List observations.

The Final Report

After the trip has taken place and students have their summarized data in front of them, they can begin to assemble and write the final report. As stated in Chapter 3, students should know prior to the field study what is expected of them for the final product. They might not have understood all that was being asked of them at that time, but once the class has completed the field exercises, the whole project begins to make sense and have significance.

The guidelines for writing the final report can range from extremely open-ended to very directed. We have found that the best reports come from a directed approach, whereby students must answer specific questions regarding forest issues, including their value and management implications. Students' responses must be based on the data they collected during the field session. To give more focus to students' management recommendations, you might give each student team a set of landowner objectives. For example:

- Imagine that the woods you measured is owned by a couple who want it managed for multiple objectives: some timber, wildlife, mushrooms, hiking, and scenic beauty.
- Imagine that your woods is owned by a ageney products company whose primary objective is timber production. The company also rents the land to a hunting club, so wildlife habitat is important, too.

Other landowners—such as a state or national forest or a Native American tribe—might have slightly different objectives. To add interest, give the landowners hypothetical names; students really like that sort of thing.

An example of the guidelines for writing a final report on the field study follows, although each instructor is free to develop his or her own format.

Final Report Guidelines

Upon completion of this study, you will construct a report that includes the following sections:

- Introduction to the Field Study
- Vegetative Analysis (overhead & vertical views)
- Study Plot Data Sheets from both study plots
  - Age Class Analysis
  - Abiotic and Biotic Environments
  - Stand Density
  - Sawtimber Inventory
  - Recreation
  - Wildlife Habitat
- Discussion of Data: Answer the following questions to guide your discussion. Assume that your study plots are a true representation of the forest types in which they were located (may or may not be true).
  1. Construct a chart comparing the abiotic variables—light intensity, temperatures, relative humidity, and wind speed—in each plot.
  2. Compare the canopy cover data from your two study plots. How does canopy cover in each plot relate to
     - the overhead view and vertical structure drawings you made?
     - ground cover density?
     - abiotic variables?
  3. What types of tree species—based on their tolerance ranking (see Appendix D)—would you expect to germinate and become established in your study plots? Any clues from the age-class analysis?
  4. *Optional*: How do the abiotic data compare between the forested plots and an adjacent open area?
  5. In which forest type that you measured would a forest fire be most likely? Why?

6. Compare the current spacing (S) for your plots and the optimum spacing for maximum wood production (S_1). If trees should be cut (thinned out), how many and which trees would you select (i.e., what would your prescription be for maximum saw timber production)?

7. Which of your study plots has produced the most board foot volume? Can you speculate why?

8. What is the commercial value of the sawtimber in your plots? (Note: You will have to visit or call a local lumberyard or building supply store to get the dollar value per board foot of the tree species in your plots. Such information also may be available on the internet, but a visit is better.)

9. What could be done to enhance or expand recreational opportunities in your overall forest area?

10. Which of your forest types would you expect to provide the best wildlife habitat? Why? How does your answer compare to your actual wildlife observations?

11. If you prescribed a thinning in either forest type, how would it affect wildlife?

12. How could you effectively manage the forests you measured to maximize the key forest values that the hypothetical landowner wants (usually timber production, wildlife habitat, and recreation)?

13. Are you aware of any controversies in your area regarding forests and their management? If so, has this exercise changed your viewpoint on these controversies?

14. Finally, what was the best part of this study? The worst? Give reasons why. How could this field study be improved?

APPENDIXES

APPENDIX A
Society of American Foresters Accredited Undergraduate Forestry Degree Programs in the United States[1]

Alabama

Auburn University
School of Forestry & Wildlife Sciences
www.forestry.auburn.edu

Alaska

University of Alaska Fairbanks
School of Natural Resources & Agricultural Sciences
www.luaf.edu/snras

Arizona

Northern Arizona University
School of Forestry
www.for.nau.edu

Arkansas

University of Arkansas at Monticello
Arkansas Forest Resources Center
www.afrc.uamont.edu

California

California Polytechnic State University
Natural Resources Management Department
www.nrm.calpoly.edu/fnr/index.ldm

Humboldt State University
Department of Forestry & Wildlife Resources
www.humboldt.edu/~for

University of California
College of Natural Resouces
www.cnr.berkeley.edu

---

[1]List is also available online at *www.safnet.org/education/handout2009Accr.pdf.*

Society of American Foresters Accredited Undergraduate Forestry Degree Programs in the United States

Colorado

> Colorado State University
> Warner College of Natural Resources
> *www.cnr.colostate.edu*

Florida

> University of Florida
> School of Forest Resources and Conservation
> *www.sfrc.ufl.edu*

Georgia

> University of Georgia
> Daniel B. Warnell School of Forestry and Natural Resources
> *www.warnell.uga.edu*

Idaho

> University of Idaho
> College of Natural Resources
> *www.uidaho.edu/cfwr*

Illinois

> Southern Illinois University Carbondale
> Department of Forestry
> *www.Coas.siu.edu*

> University of Illinois at Urbana-Champaign
> Department of Natural Resources and Environmental Sciences
> *www.aces.uiuc.edu/~nres*

Indiana

> Purdue University
> Department of Forestry and Natural Resources
> *www.ag.purdue.edu/fnr*

Society of American Foresters Accredited Undergraduate Forestry Degree Programs in the United States

Iowa

Iowa State University
Department of Natural Resource Ecology and Management
www.nrem.iastate.edu

Kentucky

University of Kentucky
College of Agriculture, Department of Forestry
www.uky.edu/Agriculture/Forestry/forestry.html

Louisiana

Louisiana State University
School of Renewable Natural Resources
www.fwf./su.edu

Louisiana Tech University
School of Forestry
www.latech.edu/ans/forestry-index.html

Maine

University of Maine
College of Natural Sciences, Forestry, and Agriculture
www.nsfa.umaine.edu

Massachusetts

University of Massachusetts, Amherst
Department of Natural Resources Conservation
http://nrc.umass.edu

Michigan

Michigan State University
Department of Forestry
www.for.msu.edu

Michigan Technological University
School of Forest Resources and Environmental Science
http://forestry.mtu.edu

Minnesota

University of Minnesota
College of Food, Agricultural and Natural Sciences
www.cfans.umn.edu

Mississippi

Mississippi State University
College of Forest Resources
www.cfr.msstate.edu

Missouri

University of Missouri
School of Natural Resources
www.snr.missouri.edu

New Hampshire

University of New Hampshire
Department of Natural Resources and the Environment
www.nre.unh.edu

New York

State University of New York
College of Environmental Science and Forestry
www.esf.edu

North Carolina

Duke University
Nicholas School of the Environment
www.env.duke.edu

North Carolina State University
Department of Forest and Environmental Resources
www.cfr.ncsu.edu/fer

Ohio

> The Ohio State University
> School of Environment & Natural Resources
> *http://senr.osu.edu*

Oklahoma

> Oklahoma State University
> Department of Natural Resource Ecology and Management
> *http://nrem.okstate.edu*

Oregon

> Oregon State University
> College of Forestry
> *http://web.cof.orst.edu*

Pennsylvania

> Pennsylvania State University
> School of Forest Resources
> *www.sfr.cas.psu.edu*

South Carolina

> Clemson University
> College of Agriculture, Forestry and Life Sciences
> *www.clemson.edu/cafls*

Tennessee

> University of Tennessee
> Department of Forestry, Wildlife and Fisheries
> *http://fwf.ag.utk.edu*

Texas

> Stephen F. Austin State University
> Arthur Temple College of Forestry and Agriculture
> *http://forestry.sfasu.edu*

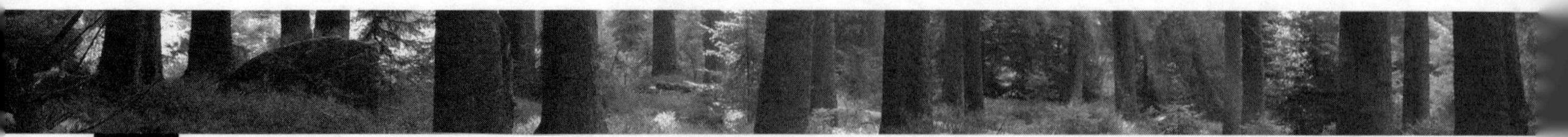

Texas A&M University
Department of Ecosystem Science & Management
http://forestry.tamu.edu

Utah

Utah State University
College of Natural Resources
www.cnr.usu.edu

Virginia

Virginia Polytechnic Institute and State University
School of Natural Resources
www.fw.vt.edu

Washington

University of Washington
School of Forest Resources
www.cfr.washington.edu

Washington State University
Department of Natural Resource Sciences
http://academic.cahnrs.wsu.edu/majors/natural-resource.html

West Virginia

West Virginia University
Davis College of Agriculture, Forestry,
and Consumer Sciences
www.davis.wvu.edu

Wisconsin

University of Wisconsin-Madison
Department of Forest and Wildlife Ecology
http://forest.wisc.edu

University of Wisconsin-Stevens Point
College of Natural Resources
www.uwsp.edu/news/uwspcatalog/CNR.htm

APPENDIX B-1
Glossary of Select Ecology and Forestry Terms[1]

Term	Definition
Advance reproduction	Young seedlings and saplings that have naturally established under an overstory canopy
Canopy	The more or less continuous cover of branches and foliage formed by the crowns of adjacent trees in a forest
Codominant	Trees in an even-aged stand, somewhat smaller than the dominants, that occupy a secondary position in the upper canopy
Conifer or coniferous tree	A needle- and cone-bearing tree, usually evergreen (e.g., pine, fir, spruce, hemlock)
Crown	The branches and foliage of a tree
Dominant	The largest trees in a stand that occupy the uppermost layer of the main canopy
Even-aged stand	A forest in which the overstory trees were established within a short period of time and are, therefore, approximately the same age.
Hardwood, broadleaf, or deciduous tree	A leaf-bearing tree that usually loses its foliage in autumn (e.g., oak, maple, ash, gum, poplar)
Intermediate	Trees of declining vigor that occupy the lowest level of the main canopy
Merchantable height	The height above the stump to which a tree stem is salable
Overstory	Those large trees in a forest that form the uppermost layer of the canopy
Pioneer	Any plant capable of invading the bare ground of a drastically disturbed area
Pole	A young tree > 4 inches but < 10 inches DBH that is just reaching commercial size (the exact limits may vary from place to place)
Sapling	A young tree > 1 inch but < 4 inches DBH
Sawlog	A log suitable in size (usually >10 inches diameter at the large end) and quality for sawing into boards.
Sawtimber	Trees 10 inches (depending on locality) or greater in DBH; trees that can be sawn into boards
Secondary succession	The process whereby pioneer vegetation becomes reestablished on a drastically disturbed area
Seedling	A very young tree < 1 inch DBH; often referred to as regeneration or reproduction
Stand	A group of trees and associated vegetation growing in an area of similar soil and climatic conditions and having a common structure and species composition

---

[1] See also the *Dictionary of Forestry*, published online by the Society of American Foresters (*www.dictionaryofforestry.org*).

Stratified stand	The vertical arrangement of trees of different heights in distinct superposed stories
Subcanopy	The cover of branches and foliage formed by the crowns of small trees growing under the main overstory canopy
Superdominant	Very large trees whose crowns project above the main layer of the canopy
Suppressed	Small trees of low vigor in an even-aged stand growing just below the main canopy
Tolerance	See Appendix D
Thinning	A timber harvest in a stand—i.e., a reduction in stand density—designed to open up growing space for the remaining trees
Understory	Trees and shrubs growing under an overstory, usually the lowest stratum in a forest
Uneven-aged stand	A forest where trees of markedly different ages intermingle, producing a complex structure of many strata

Unit	Definition
Wood Volume	
Board foot	A piece of sawn wood 1 foot × 1 foot × 1 inch thick
Cord	A pile of stacked wood 4 feet × 4 feet × 8 feet = 128 cubic feet
Face cord	A pile of stacked firewood 4 feet × 8 feet × ca. 16 inches long (or whatever length has been cut)
Cunit	100 cubic feet
Cubic meter (m³)	35.3 cubic feet or 424 board feet
Length or Height	
Bolt	A small-diameter log 8 feet or 100 inches long
Log	A large-diameter log 16 feet long
Half log	A large-diameter log 8 feet long
Meter (m)	3.28 feet
Girth	
DBH	Tree trunk diameter at breast height—4.5 feet or 1.4 meters above the ground—in inches or centimeters
Basal area (BA)	Tree trunk area at breast height in square inches or square meters $1 \text{ in}^2 = 0.093 \text{ m}^2$
Land Area	
Acre	43,560 square feet
Section	640 acres or 1 square mile (more or less)
Milacre	1/1000 of an acre; equals a square 6.6 feet on a side or a circle with a radius of 3.7 feet
Hectare (ha)	2.54 acres

For efficiency and to avoid conflicts, each team of five or six students should have their own set of equipment. This will allow them to complete the activities in the field independent of other groups. Some of the equipment may be obtained locally; the rest can be purchased online from forestry or natural resource supply companies, such as Forestry Suppliers (*www. forestry-suppliers.com*) or Ben Meadows (*www.benmeadows.com*).

Per team (5 to 6 students):

- 1 large plastic tub with lid (numbered) to store all equipment
- 1 digital temperature probe (for air and soil temperature)
- 1 sling psychrometer (hygrometer) for relative humidity
- 1 digital light meter (measure in Lux)
- 1 anemometer for wind velocity
- 1 GRS densitometer for determining tree canopy
- 1 3.3- × 3.3-foot subplot marker constructed with ¾-inch PVC pipe and elbows to determine ground cover density
- 1 small plastic screw-top bottle with distilled water (for hygrometer)
- 1 tree and log scale stick to determine DBH, number of logs, and standing board feet
- 1 tree caliper or diameter tape to be used in stocking and age class analysis
- 1 20- to 25-foot carpenter's measuring tape
- 3 rolls of different-color biodegradeable flagging
- One copy of a field guide to trees in the area (see Appendix E for examples)
- 5 or 6 clipboards
- 5 or 6 pairs of safety glasses
- 5 or 6 hard hats (recommended)
- Insect repellant
- Equipment list (plastic laminated)

The equipment listed above represents an economical approach that minimizes costs. More sophisticated equipment is available but at greater expense. Most of the equipment is not consumable and therefore should have considerable longevity.

Funding for forestry field studies may involve the writing of grants or requests to your school's parent-teacher organization. You also may be able to secure donations from local lumber companies, home supply stores, forest products industries, forestry organizations (e.g., the local chapter of the Society of American Foresters), or community organizations. The key is to present a prospective donor with a clear, concise, and enthusiastic summary of what you want to do, perhaps targeting specific equipment needs. You do not need to ask for large sums; a few hundred dollars from a few sources might be enough to put you and your students on the road to the nearest woods.

APPENDIX D
Tolerance[a] Ranking of Select North American Tree Species[b]

Common Name	Latin Name	Tolerance Ranking
Alaska-yellow cedar	*Chamaecyparis nootkatensis*	Tolerant
Alpine larch	*Larix lyallii*	Very intolerant
American basswood	*Tilia americana*	Tolerant
American beech	*Fagus grandifolia*	Very tolerant
American elm	*Ulmus americana*	Intermediate
Atlantic white-cedar	*Chamaecyparis thyoides*	Intermediate
Baldcypress	*Taxodium distichum var. distichum*	Intermediate
Balsam fir	*Abies balsamea*	Very tolerant
Balsam poplar	*Populus balsamifera*	Very intolerant
Bigleaf maple	*Acer macrophyllum*	Very tolerant
Bigtooth aspen	*Populus grandidentata*	Very intolerant
Bitternut hickory	*Carya cordiformis*	Intolerant
Black ash	*Fraxinus nigra*	Intolerant
Black cherry	*Prunus serotina*	Intolerant
Black cottonwood	*Populus trichocarpa*	Very intolerant
Black locust	*Robinia pseudoacacia*	Very intolerant
Black maple	*Acer nigrum*	Very intolerant
Black oak	*Quercus velutina*	Intermediate
Black spruce	*Picea mariana*	Tolerant
Black tupelo	*Nyssa sylvatica var. sylvatica*	Tolerant
Black walnut	*Juglans nigra*	Intolerant
Black willow	*Salix nigra*	Very intolerant
Blue spruce	*Picea pungens*	Intermediate
Bur oak	*Quercus macrocarpa*	Intermediate
Butternut	*Juglans cinerea*	Intolerant
California black oak	*Quercus kelloggii*	Intolerant
California red fir	*Abies magnifica*	Tolerant
Canyon live oak	*Quercus chrysolepis*	Tolerant
Cherrybark oak	*Quercus falcata var. pagodifolia*	Intolerant
Chestnut oak	*Quercus prinus*	Intermediate
Chinkapin oak	*Quercus muehlenbergii*	Intolerant
Common persimmon	*Diospyros virginiana*	Very tolerant
Cucumber tree	*Magnolia acuminata*	Intermediate

Tolerance[a] Ranking of Select North American Tree Species[b]

Douglas fir	*Pseudotsuga menziesii*	Intermediate
Eastern cottonwood	*Populus deltoides*	Very intolerant
Eastern hemlock	*Tsuga canadensis*	Very tolerant
Eastern hophornbeam	*Ostrya virginiana*	Tolerant
Eastern red cedar	*Juniperus virginiana*	Intol.-Very Intol.
Eastern white pine	*Pinus strobus*	Intermediate
Engelmann spruce	*Picea engelmannii*	Tolerant
Flowering dogwood	*Cornus florida*	Very tolerant
Fraser fir	*Abies fraseri*	Very tolerant
Giant chinkapin	*Castanopsis chrysophylla*	Intermediate
Giant sequoia	*Sequoiadendron giganteum*	Intolerant
Grand fir	*Abies grandis*	Tolerant
Green ash	*Fraxinus pennsylvanica*	Tolerant
Hackberry	*Celtis occidentalis*	Intermediate
Honeylocust	*Gleditsia triacanthos*	Intolerant
Incense-cedar	*Libocedrus decurrens*	Intermediate
Jack pine	*Pinus banksiana*	Intolerant
Jeffrey pine	*Pinus jeffreyi*	Intolerant
Laurel oak	*Quercus laurifolia*	Tolerant
Live oak	*Quercus virginiana*	Intermediate
Loblolly pine	*Pinus taeda*	Intolerant
Lodgepole pine	*Pinus contorta*	Very intolerant
Longleaf pine	*Pinus palustris*	Intolerant
Mockernut hickory	*Carya tomentosa*	Intolerant
Monterey pine	*Pinus radiata*	Intermediate
Mountain hemlock	*Tsuga mertensiana*	Tolerant
Nuttall oak	*Quercus nuttallii*	Intolerant
Ohio buckeye	*Aesculus glabra*	Tolerant
Oregon ash	*Fraxinus latifolia*	Intermediate
Oregon white oak	*Quercus garryana*	Intolerant
Osage-orange	*Maclura pomifera*	Intolerant
Overcup oak	*Quercus lyrata*	Intermediate
Pacific madrone	*Arbutus menziesii*	Intermediate
Pacific silver fir	*Abies amabilis*	Very tolerant
Pacific yew	*Taxus brevifolia*	Very tolerant

Tolerance[a] Ranking of Select North American Tree Species[b]

Paper birch	Betula papyrifera	Intolerant
Pecan	Carya illinoensis	Intolerant
Pignut hickory	Carya glabra	Intermediate
Pin cherry	Prunus pensylvanica	Very intolerant
Pin oak	Quercus palustris	Intolerant
Pinyon	Pinus edulis	Intolerant
Pitch pine	Pinus rigida	Intolerant
Pondcypress	Taxodium distichum var. nutans	Intermediate
Ponderosa pine	Pinus ponderosa	Intolerant
Pond pine	Pinus serotina	Intolerant
Port-Orford-cedar	Charnaecyparis lawsoniana	Tolerant
Post oak	Quercus stellata	Intolerant
Quaking aspen	Populus tremuloides	Very intolerant
Red alder	Alnus rubra	Intolerant
Red maple	Acer rubrum	Tolerant
Red mulberry	Morus rubra	Tolerant
Red pine	Pinus resinosa.	Intolerant
Red spruce	Picea rubens	Very tolerant
Redwood	Sequoia sempervirens	Very tolerant
River birch	Betula nigra	Intolerant
Rock elm	Ulmus thomasii	Intermediate
Rocky Mountain juniper	Juniperus scopulorum	Very intolerant
Sand pine	Pinus clausa	Intermediate
Sassafras	Sassafras albidum	Intolerant
Scarlet oak	Quercus coccinea	Very intolerant
Shagbark hickory	Carya ovata	Intermediate
Shellbark hickory	Carya laciniosa	Very tolerant
Sitka spruce	Picea sitchensis	Tolerant
Slash pine	Pinus elliottii	Intolerant
Slippery elm	Ulmus rubra	Tolerant
Sourwood	Oxydendrum arboreum	Tolerant
Southern magnolia	Magnolia grandiflora	Tolerant
Southern red oak	Quercus falcata var. falcata	Intermediate
Spruce pine	Pinus glabra	Very tolerant
Subalpine fir	Abies lasiocarpa	Tolerant

Tolerance[a] Ranking of Select North American Tree Species[b]

Sugar maple	*Acer saccharum*	Very tolerant
Sugar pine	*Pinus lambertiana*	Intermediate
Swamp chestnut oak	*Quercus michauxii*	Intolerant
Swamp cottonwood	*Populus heterophylla*	Intolerant
Swamp white oak	*Quercus bicolor*	Intermediate
Sweet birch	*Betula lenta*	Intolerant
Sweetgum	*Liquidambar styraciflua*	Intolerant
Sycamore	*Platanus occidentalis*	Intermediate
Tamarack	*Larix laricina*	Very intolerant
Tanoak	*Lithocarpus densiflorus*	Tolerant
Turkey oak	*Quercus laevis*	Intolerant
Virginia pine	*Pinus virginiana*	Intolerant
Water oak	*Quercus nigra*	Intolerant
Water tupelo	*Nyssa aquatica.*	Intolerant
Western hemlock	*Tsuga heterophylla*	Very tolerant
Western juniper	*Juniperus occidentalis*	Intolerant
Western larch	*Larix occidentalis*	Very intolerant
Western red cedar	*Thuja plicata*	Very tolerant
Western white pine	*Pinus monticola*	Intermediate
White ash	*Fraxinus americana*	Intolerant
White basswood	*Tilia heterophylla*	Tolerant
White fir	*Abies concolor*	Tolerant
White oak	*Quercus alba*	Intermediate
White spruce	*Picea glauca*	Intermediate
Whitebark pine	*Pinus albicaulis*	Intermediate
Willow oak	*Quercus phellos*	Intolerant
Winged elm	*Ulmus alata*	Tolerant
Yellow birch	*Betula alleghaniensis*	Intermediate
Yellow buckeye	*Aesculus octandra*	Tolerant
Yellow-poplar	*Liriodendron tulipifera*	Intolerant

[a]*Tolerance* is defined as the ability to survive and grow in the shade of and in competition with other trees. Very tolerant trees can bear deep shade, whereas intolerant trees demand full or nearly full light.

[b] Modified from Burns, R. M. and B. H. Honkala. 1965. *Silvics of North America. http://www.na.fs. fed.us/spfo/pubs/silvics_manual/table_of_contents.htm.*

Many books, scientific papers, field guides, and bulletins on forestry, ecology, and environmental subjects have been published over the years. The following list represents some publications—in addition to those cited in the reference lists for Chapters 1 and 2—that may be helpful and interesting. Two textbooks recommended for Advanced Placement Environmental Science also are included.

In addition, information and help on forest-related subjects is readily available on the internet. Especially helpful are publications from state extension services, many of which can be downloaded in PDF format. Plug the subject that interests you into your favorite search engine and see what you get! But remember, books and bulletins from commercial publishing houses, academic institutions, professional and scientific organizations, and natural resource agencies have been subjected to technical and editorial reviews to ensure their accuracy, relevance, and authenticity; many documents posted on the internet have not—reader beware.

Benyus, J. M. 1989. *The field guide to wildlife habitats of the Eastern United States*. New York: Fireside.

Botkin, D. B., and E. A. Keller. 2007. *Environmental science: Earth as a living planet*. 6th ed. New York: John Wiley & Sons.

Brockman, C. F., and R. Marrilees. 2001. *Trees of North America: A guide to field identification*, revised ed. New York: St. Martin's Press, Golden Field Guide.

Leopold, A. 1986. *A sand county almanac*. New York: Ballantine Books.

Little, E. L. 1980. *National Audubon Society field guide to North American Trees—Eastern region*. New York: Alfred A. Knopf.

Little, E. L. 1980. *National Audubon Society field guide to North American trees—Western region*. New York: Alfred A. Knopf.

Mitchell, M. K., and W. B. Stapp. 2008. *Field manual for water quality monitoring: An environmental education program for schools*. 12th ed. Dubuque, IA: Kendall Hunt.

Raven, P. H., L. R. Berg, and D. M. Hassenzahl. 2008. *Environment*. 6th ed. New York: John Wiley & Sons.

We highly recommend the exceptionally user-friendly and well-illustrated books in the **Peterson Field Guide Series** published by Houghton Mifflin Harcourt. The books cover just about every aspect of the natural world. Roger Tory Peterson was one of the world's preeminent naturalists, and his identification system has been called the greatest invention for nature watchers since binoculars.

David D. Glenn is a retired teacher from Rochester Hills, Michigan, where he taught Conservation of Natural Resources, Advanced Placement Environmental Science, Tropical Ecology, and Ecology of Greater Yellowstone—among other advanced courses—at Adams High School. Mr. Glenn holds a bachelor's degree from Central Michigan University and a master's degree from Michigan State University. During his 35-year teaching career, Mr. Glenn was awarded the Presidential Award for Excellence in Science and Mathematics Teaching and the National Association of Biology Teachers' Ecology/Environmental Science Teaching Award, among other honors.

Donald I. Dickmann holds a bachelor's degree in forest management from the University of Washington and a PhD in plant physiology from the University of Wisconsin. His duty stations have included the U.S. Forest Service North Central Research Station, West Georgia College, Iowa State University, and—for 35 years—the Department of Forestry at Michigan State University. During his 39-year teaching career, Dr. Dickmann taught undergraduate and graduate courses in biology, botany, plant physiology, silviculture, wildland fire, tree physiology, forest ecology, dendrology, forestry research, and general forestry. He is the author of 120 scientific papers, articles, and bulletins, as well as five books. He is a certified forester and a fellow of the Society of American Foresters.

INDEX

INDEX

INDEX

NATIONAL SCIENCE TEACHERS ASSOCIATION